Betty Crocker

Make It in One

Dinner in One Pan, One Pot, One Sheet Pan ... and More

Houghton Mifflin Harcourt
Boston • New York

GENERAL MILLS

Global Business Solutions Director:
Heather Polen

Global Business Solutions Manager:
Andrea Kleinschmit

Executive Editor:
Cathy Swanson Wheaton

Recipe Development and Testing:
Betty Crocker Kitchens

Photography: General Mills
Photography Studios and Image Library

HOUGHTON MIFFLIN HARCOURT

Editorial Director: Deb Brody

Executive Editor: Anne Ficklen

Editorial Associate: Sarah Kwak

Managing Editor: Marina Padakis

Production Editor: Kiffin Steurer

Cover Design: Tai Blanche

Art Director & Book Design:
Tai Blanche

Senior Production Coordinator:
Kimberly Kiefer

Find more great ideas at
BettyCrocker.com

For information about permission to reproduce selections from this book, write to Permissions, Houghton Mifflin Harcourt Publishing Company, 3 Park Avenue, New York, New York 10016.

www.hmhbooks.com

Library of Congress Cataloging-in-Publication Data:

Names: Houghton Mifflin Harcourt Publishing Company, publisher.

Title: Betty Crocker make it in one : dinner in one pan, one pot, one sheet pan ... and more.

Other titles: Make it in one : dinner in one pan, one pot, one sheet pan ...and more

Description: Boston : Houghton Mifflin Harcourt, 2019.

Identifiers: LCCN 2018036023 (print) | LCCN 2018038316 (ebook) | ISBN 9781328587602 (ebook) | ISBN 9781328588777 (trade paper)

Subjects: LCSH: One-dish meals. | Electric cooking, Slow. | Pressure cooking.| Quick and easy cooking. | LCGFT: Cookbooks.

Classification: LCC TX840.O53 (ebook) | LCC TX840.O53 B49 2019 (print) | DDC 641.82—dc23

LC record available at https://lccn.loc.gov/2018036023

Printed in the United States of America

LBC 10 9 8 7 6 5 4 3

4500756054

Cover photos: Easy Sausage Lasagna (page 97), Lemon Chicken and Potatoes (page 116)

Dear Busy Cooks

We know how hard it is getting food on the table amid a flurry of evening activities. How do you make dinner and clean up, and still make it to soccer practice? Recipes made in only one vessel is our secret. They're as easy to make as they are to clean up!

From skillet and big pot meals to complete meals made in a slow cooker or Instant Pot, on a sheet pan or using other familiar pans, this delicious collection will be sure to come to your rescue again and again. From comforting favorites like Favorite Chicken Nuggets to new family favorites like Chicken Sausage and Mini Pepper Pizza, there's a wide variety to tantalize your taste buds. Look for these recipes when you're crunched for time:

- **Quick Prep: ready to cook in 20 minutes or less**

- **Done in 30 minutes or less**

We've made customizability the heart of these recipes. Look for our **Customize It** tips with many of them, as well as terrific features that extend your creativity even further. **Clever, No-Fuss Pizza Crusts, Stuffed Peppers 4 Ways and Let's Oven-Fry** features zero-in-on fabulous ways to make your meals different every time.

And if you want to take Meatless Mondays further into the week, check out a variety of meatless recipes we offer throughout the book. Our **Make It Meatless** feature showcases ways to transform your meat-based recipe into meatless wonders, with inexpensive, simple substitutions and tips.

Your family's *mmms* and *ahhs* will bring you joy when you serve these yummy recipes. Then tidy up in a flash and get on to your evening!

Your Friend,

Betty Crocker

Contents

....

The Wonders of One-Pot Cooking

One-pot cooking takes the pressure off getting dinner on the table! You need only one vessel to cook in; therefore, you have only one to clean up, getting you out of the kitchen and back to your busy life! Depending on how hungry your bunch is, these delicious, satisfying recipes can mostly stand on their own . . . one dish and dinner's done.

Look below for fabulous tips and tricks we've learned in the Betty Crocker Test Kitchens for making these terrific one-pot meals:

Instant Pot™ Success

What exactly is an Instant Pot? It's like a combination slow cooker and pressure cooker with the ability to sauté, which can save you more dishes, steps and time than recipes cooked with other methods. To understand the proper use of your multi-use programmable pressure cooker and how to cook safely, refer to your owner's manual. Here's what we've learned from developing recipes using these appliances:

GENERAL GUIDELINES

- Start with reputable, kitchen-tested recipes to ensure you end up with great results. These appliances are not forgiving like a slow cooker, since you must release the pressure before you check for doneness and shouldn't add extra time after that due to food safety and safe-handling reasons.
- The Instant Pot is great for tough cuts such as brisket and shoulder (where the meat will be shredded). Bone-in pork chops work better than boneless chops, and the fat in chicken thighs helps them turn out better than leaner chicken breasts. Smaller cuts of meat work well in stews and chilis.
- Foods generally take about 13 to 15 minutes to get to the correct pressure before the programmed buttons

start to cook and count down the indicated time. There is also time for the pressure to release once the cooking program is finished. This time is reflected in the total (Start to Finish) times on our recipes.

- For some types of recipes, the Instant Pot can cut down on cooking time as compared with other appliances. For other types of recipes, the cooking time plus the time it takes to build up the proper pressure and then release it at the end can end up about the same as with other cooking methods.
- Instant Pot recipes cannot be used interchangeably with stove top pressure cookers as they don't perform with the same pressure.
- Don't fill your Instant Pot past the indicator line (usually about two-thirds full for most recipes or half full for foods that expand in size, such rice) for best results.
- At least 1 cup of liquid is needed for the food to be able to get to the correct pressure to cook.

SAUTÉING AND BROWNING IN THE INSTANT POT

- Sauté is a great feature of multi-use programmable pressure cookers, which allow recipes to be made in them without needing another pot to cook in first. Generally, select **NORMAL** for the correct heat temperature for browning. Be sure to always press **CANCEL** and then reprogram for the next step after that. You cannot go directly from **SAUTÉ** to **MANUAL** or **PRESSURE COOK**.

- You can brown meat in the Instant Pot using the **SAUTÉ** feature. To brown meat, depending on the cut, you may need to do it in 2 or 3 batches. This way, the cooking juices have a chance to evaporate rather than steam the meat and discolor the finished dish.

- If small bits are left in the bottom of your Instant Pot after sautéing, the sensor may notice them and indicate that it's burning when it isn't. Be sure to use the amount of liquid called for in the recipe, and stir up any bits from the bottom of the Instant Pot after sautéing in it.

- After your food is cooked, the **SAUTÉ** feature can also be used to thicken the sauce or to cook noodles for the dish.

RELEASING PRESSURE

- Recipes use either manual/quick release of pressure or natural release, depending on the type of food being cooked. **Manual/quick release** (usually about 5 minutes) releases pressure quickly for foods that need to halt the cooking process. **Natural release** (about 30 minutes) releases pressure slowly, allowing food such as tough meat cuts to continue cooking and become more tender while the pressure drops.

- Instant Pots with pressure valves show visually when the steam has been released. For those that don't have pressure valves, pressure is released when steam no longer is coming out of the unit. Do not attempt to open the lid until the pressure has completely released.

- Meats may look dry when removed from the appliance but will be moist when eaten if cooked properly. You can baste the cooked meat with a little of the cooking juices to alleviate the dry appearance.

- Since there is no release of moisture, the texture of rice and pasta isn't quite the same when cooked with other methods.

Slow-Cooker Success

Use these tips to ensure great results from your slow cooker:

- Spray the inside of the insert or cooker with cooking spray for easy cleanup.

- Slow cookers work most efficiently when two-thirds to three-fourths full.

- Always keep the slow cooker covered for the specified cooking time. Each time the lid is removed, it allows heat to escape, adding 15 to 20 minutes to the cooking time. Exception: large cuts of meat should be rotated halfway through cooking for best results.

- Root vegetables take longer to cook than other vegetables, so cut them smaller and put them on the bottom of the cooker.

- Cover raw potatoes with liquid to prevent them from turning dark.

SLOW-COOKER SAFETY

Slow cookers heat up more slowly and cook at lower temperatures than do other appliances. To keep food safe, follow these guidelines:

- Use ingredients that are completely thawed.

- Keep perishable foods refrigerated until you are ready to put them in the cooker.

- Always cook and drain ground meat just before placing it in the cooker—not ahead of time.

- Brown poultry and meats just before placing them in the cooker—not ahead of time.

- Whole chickens can be cooked in a slow cooker if they are 4½ lb or smaller and cooked in a 5- to 6-quart slow cooker, so that they have enough room and can reach the proper temperature quickly enough.

- To ensure that the dish cooks properly, follow recipes exactly for specific sizes when cutting ingredients and for layering.

- Place leftovers in shallow containers and refrigerate within 2 hours of cooking. Don't use the insert for storage.

- Always reheat foods with your microwave, conventional oven or stovetop before placing in the slow cooker to keep warm until serving. Don't use a slow cooker for heating up food.

Skillet

Cilantro-Lime Chicken and Rice

Prep Time: 35 Minutes • Start to Finish: 1 Hour 5 Minutes • 6 servings

CHICKEN AND RICE

- 1 package (0.85 oz) chicken taco seasoning mix
- ¼ teaspoon ground red pepper (cayenne)
- 4 boneless skinless chicken breasts (1½ lb)
- 1 tablespoon vegetable oil
- 2¼ cups chicken broth (from 32-oz carton)
- 2 tablespoons lime juice
- 1 tablespoon finely chopped garlic
- 1 cup uncooked regular long-grain white rice
- 1 cup canned black beans, drained, rinsed
- 1 can (4.5 oz) chopped green chiles

TOPPING AND GARNISH

- ¼ cup water
- 2 tablespoons lime juice
- 1 medium avocado, pitted, peeled and cut into 1-inch pieces
- ¼ cup chopped fresh cilantro
- 1 teaspoon finely chopped garlic
- ⅛ teaspoon salt

  Chopped fresh cilantro and lime wedges

1. In large resealable food-storage plastic bag, combine taco seasoning mix and red pepper. Add chicken to bag, seal and shake to coat chicken evenly.

2. In 12-inch nonstick skillet, heat oil over medium-high heat. Cook chicken in oil 5 to 7 minutes, turning once, until browned on both sides. Remove chicken from skillet; cover to keep warm.

3. To same skillet, add remaining chicken and rice ingredients; heat to boiling. Cover; reduce heat to medium-low. Simmer 12 to 15 minutes or until liquid has been reduced by about half. Stir mixture thoroughly; place chicken on top of rice.

4. Cover; cook 12 to 15 minutes or until juice of chicken is clear when center of thickest part is cut (at least 165°F) and rice is tender. Place chicken on cutting board. Cut chicken into ½-inch slices; return to skillet.

5. Meanwhile, in mini food processor or blender, place all topping ingredients. Process until smooth, scraping down sides of processor as necessary. Transfer mixture to small resealable food-storage plastic bag. Cut corner from one end; squeeze topping on sliced chicken and rice before serving.

6. Garnish with chopped cilantro and lime wedges. Serve any remaining topping with chicken and rice.

1 Serving: Calories 400; Total Fat 11g (Saturated Fat 2g, Trans Fat 0g); Cholesterol 80mg; Sodium 910mg; Total Carbohydrate 41g (Dietary Fiber 5g); Protein 35g **Exchanges:** 2½ Starch, 4 Very Lean Meat, 1½ Fat **Carbohydrate Choices:** 3

Customize It If desired, stir ¼ teaspoon ground red pepper into the rice for a delicious bit of additional heat.

Make It a Meal Serve this southwestern-flavored dish with sliced avocado and tomato wedges.

Caprese Chicken and Orzo

Prep Time: 20 Minutes • Start to Finish: 40 Minutes • 4 servings

4   boneless skinless chicken breasts (1¼ lb)

1   teaspoon salt

½   teaspoon pepper

2   tablespoons olive oil

1   cup chicken broth (from 32-oz carton)

1   can (14.5 oz) fire-roasted diced tomatoes, undrained

1   cup uncooked orzo or rosamarina pasta (6 oz)

1   package (8 oz) fresh mozzarella cheese pearls, drained

¼   cup shredded fresh basil leaves

1 Sprinkle both sides of chicken with ½ teaspoon of the salt and the pepper.

2 In 12-inch nonstick skillet, heat oil over medium-high heat. Add chicken; cook 3 to 4 minutes on each side or until browned. Remove chicken from skillet; place on plate.

3 Add broth, tomatoes and remaining ½ teaspoon salt to skillet; heat to boiling. Stir in orzo; return to boiling. Place chicken on orzo.

4 Reduce heat to medium-low; cover and simmer 12 to 16 minutes or until most of liquid is absorbed, orzo is tender and juice of chicken is clear when center of thickest part is cut (at least 165°F).

5 Top mixture with mozzarella pearls; cover, cook over medium-low heat 2 to 4 minutes or until mozzarella slightly melts. Sprinkle with basil.

1 Serving: Calories 560; Total Fat 23g (Saturated Fat 2.5g, Trans Fat 0g); Cholesterol 140mg; Sodium 1210mg; Total Carbohydrate 34g (Dietary Fiber 2g); Protein 53g **Exchanges:** 2½ Starch, 5½ Lean Meat, 1 Medium-Fat Meat **Carbohydrate Choices:** 2

Customize It Mozzarella cheese pearls are available at many supermarkets near the other cheese items. If they are not available, shredded mozzarella is a nice substitute.

Hawaiian Chicken

Prep Time: 20 Minutes • Start to Finish: 50 Minutes • 5 servings (about 1¼ cups each)

1 tablespoon vegetable oil

1 lb boneless skinless chicken breast halves, cut into bite-size pieces

2 medium bell peppers (any color), coarsely chopped (2 cups)

1 medium onion, cut into wedges

1 can (8 oz) pineapple chunks in juice, drained, juice reserved

1 cup uncooked regular long-grain white rice

1 cup light coconut milk (not cream of coconut)

⅔ cup chicken broth (from 32-oz carton)

¾ teaspoon salt

1 tablespoon chopped fresh cilantro

½ cup cashew halves and pieces

4 medium green onions, sliced (¼ cup)

1 In 12-inch skillet, heat oil over medium-high heat. Add chicken, bell peppers and onion; cook stirring frequently 3 to 4 minutes or until chicken is no longer pink.

2 Stir in reserved pineapple juice, rice, coconut milk, chicken broth and salt. Heat to boiling; reduce heat to low. Cover; simmer 20 to 25 minutes, stirring once, or until rice is tender and liquid is absorbed.

3 Stir in pineapple chunks and cilantro; cook until thoroughly heated. Sprinkle with cashews and green onions.

1 Serving: Calories 440; Total Fat 15g (Saturated Fat 5g, Trans Fat 0g); Cholesterol 55mg; Sodium 540mg; Total Carbohydrate 50g (Dietary Fiber 3g); Protein 27g **Exchanges:** 1½ Starch, 1½ Other Carbohydrate, ½ Vegetable, 3 Very Lean Meat, 2½ Fat **Carbohydrate Choices:** 3

Genius Tip Coconut milk is a creamy, rich liquid that adds a subtle, sweet coconut flavor. Often the heavier "cream" part rises to the top of the can and the watery "milk" goes to the bottom of the can. Pour the coconut milk into a large measuring cup or medium bowl and whisk together before adding to your dish.

Genius Tip We only cook the chicken in the first step just until the outside is no longer pink. The chicken will continue to cook as the rice cooks so everything will be done at the same time.

Saucy Chicken Parmesan

Prep Time: 25 Minutes • Start to Finish: 25 Minutes • 4 servings

¾ cup Original Bisquick® mix

1 teaspoon Italian seasoning

2 tablespoons grated Parmesan cheese

1 egg

4 boneless skinless chicken breasts (1 lb)

3 tablespoons olive or vegetable oil

2 cups tomato pasta sauce (from 26-oz jar)

1 cup shredded Italian cheese blend (4 oz)

1 In shallow dish or pie plate, combine Bisquick mix, Italian seasoning and Parmesan cheese. In another shallow dish or pie plate, beat egg. Coat chicken with Bisquick mixture; dip into egg. Coat again with Bisquick mixture.

2 In 12-inch nonstick skillet, heat oil over medium heat. Cook chicken 4 to 6 minutes, turning once, until golden brown. Cover; cook 8 to 10 minutes longer, turning once, until juice of chicken is clear when center of thickest part is cut (165°F). Remove chicken from skillet; place on plate.

3 Pour pasta sauce into skillet. Place chicken on top of sauce. Sprinkle with Italian cheese blend. Cover; cook 2 to 3 minutes or until bubbly and cheese is melted.

1 Serving: Calories 590; Total Fat 31g (Saturated Fat 10g, Trans Fat 1g); Cholesterol 145mg; Sodium 1260mg; Total Carbohydrate 39g (Dietary Fiber 2g); Protein 39g **Exchanges:** 1 Starch, 1 Other Carbohydrate, ½ Low-Fat Milk, ½ Vegetable, 4½ Lean Meat, 3 Fat **Carbohydrate Choices:** 2½

Make It a Meal For a family-pleasing Italian meal, serve this easy chicken dish with cooked spaghetti or vermicelli, broccoli and a crisp tossed salad.

Easy Mexican Chicken and Beans

Prep Time: 30 Minutes • Start to Finish: 30 Minutes • 4 servings

1 lb uncooked chicken breast strips for stir-fry

1 package (1 oz) taco seasoning mix

1 can (15 oz) black beans, drained, rinsed

1 can (11 oz) whole kernel corn with red and green peppers, undrained

¼ cup water

Flour tortillas, if desired

1 Spray 10-inch skillet with cooking spray. Add chicken to skillet; cook over medium-high heat 8 to 10 minutes, stirring occasionally, until no longer pink in center.

2 Stir in seasoning mix, beans, corn and water. Cook over medium-high heat 8 to 10 minutes, stirring frequently, until sauce is slightly thickened. Serve with tortillas.

1 Serving: Calories 340; Total Fat 5g (Saturated Fat 1g, Trans Fat 0g); Cholesterol 70mg; Sodium 1060mg; Total Carbohydrate 39g (Dietary Fiber 9g); Protein 33g **Exchanges:** 1½ Starch, 1 Other Carbohydrate, 4 Very Lean Meat, ½ Fat **Carbohydrate Choices:** 2½

Genius Tip If the stir-fry chicken strips are not available, purchase the same weight amount of boneless skinless chicken breasts or thighs, and cut into strips.

Customize It If you prefer, pinto beans can easily be substituted for the black beans.

Ranch Chicken

Prep Time: 5 Minutes • Start to Finish: 20 Minutes • 4 servings

¼ cup ranch dressing

⅓ cup seasoned or unseasoned dry bread crumbs

4 boneless skinless chicken breast halves (1 lb)

2 tablespoons olive or vegetable oil

1 Place dressing in shallow bowl. Place bread crumbs in another shallow bowl. Dip chicken into dressing; coat thoroughly with bread crumbs.

2 In 10-inch skillet, heat oil over medium-high heat. Cook chicken 12 to 15 minutes, turning once, until outside is golden brown and juice is no longer pink when centers of thickest pieces are cut (165°F).

1 Serving: Calories 360; Total Fat 19g (Saturated Fat 3.5g, Trans Fat 0g); Cholesterol 105mg; Sodium 400mg; Total Carbohydrate 7g (Dietary Fiber 0g); Protein 38g **Exchanges:** ½ Starch, 5½ Very Lean Meat, 3 Fat **Carbohydrate Choices:** ½

Make It a Meal Mashed potatoes and mixed vegetables are ideal to serve with this tasty chicken main dish.

Genius Tip Sliced or shredded leftover chicken breasts are perfect for sandwiches. Spread bread with a spoonful of cranberry relish for a sweet-tart flavor accent.

Chicken Fajita Quesadillas

Prep Time: 40 Minutes • **Start to Finish: 40 Minutes** • **8 quesadillas**

2 tablespoons lime juice

1 package (0.85 oz) chicken taco seasoning mix

3 boneless skinless chicken breasts (about 1 lb), cut into 1-inch pieces

6 teaspoons vegetable oil

2 medium bell peppers, chopped (about 2 cups)

1 medium red onion, chopped (about ½ cup)

1 package (11 oz) flour tortillas for burritos (8 tortillas, 8 inch)

2 cups shredded pepper Jack cheese (8 oz)

1 cup chunky-style salsa

½ cup sour cream

1 medium avocado, pitted, peeled and sliced

1 In small bowl, mix lime juice and taco seasoning mix; pour into gallon-size resealable food-storage plastic bag. Place chicken in bag; seal. Shake chicken until evenly coated.

2 In 12-inch nonstick skillet, heat 1 teaspoon of the oil over medium-high heat. Add bell peppers and onion; cook and stir 4 to 5 minutes or until vegetables are tender. Spoon vegetables into bowl.

3 Add 1 teaspoon of the oil to same skillet over medium heat. Add chicken; cook 4 to 6 minutes or until chicken is no longer pink in center. Transfer to bowl with vegetables. Stir to combine. Wipe skillet clean with paper towels.

4 On half of each tortilla, layer ¼ cup of the cheese and slightly less than ½ cup of the chicken and vegetable mixture. Fold each tortilla in half. Brush top of each quesadilla with about ½ teaspoon of the oil.

5 Heat 12-inch nonstick skillet over medium heat. Place 2 quesadillas in skillet, oil side down; brush top side with about ½ teaspoon of the oil. Cook about 1 minute or until light golden brown. Carefully turn quesadilla; cook 1 to 2 minutes longer or until golden brown. Repeat with remaining quesadillas. Cut each quesadilla in half; serve with salsa, sour cream and avocado.

1 Quesadilla: Calories 420; Total Fat 23g (Saturated Fat 10g, Trans Fat 1.5g); Cholesterol 70mg; Sodium 960mg; Total Carbohydrate 30g (Dietary Fiber 2g); Protein 23g **Exchanges:** 1½ Starch, ½ Other Carbohydrate, ½ Vegetable, 1½ Very Lean Meat, 1 High-Fat Meat, 2½ Fat **Carbohydrate Choices:** 2

Customize It If you like spicy quesadillas, finely chop a serrano chili, and cook with the vegetables.

Sausage-Jalapeño Popper Dinner

Prep Time: 20 Minutes • Start to Finish: 35 Minutes • 4 servings (1¼ cups each)

1 lb bulk Italian pork sausage

1 medium onion, chopped (½ cup)

2 cloves garlic, finely chopped

1 large jalapeño chile, seeded, chopped (about ¼ cup)

2 cups chicken broth (from 32-oz carton)

1 cup uncooked orzo or rosamarina pasta (6 oz)

1 green bell pepper, chopped (1 cup)

½ cup shredded Cheddar cheese (2 oz)

4 oz cream cheese, softened, cubed

Sliced jalapeño chile, if desired

1 In 12-inch skillet, cook sausage, onion, garlic and chopped chile over medium-high heat, stirring frequently, 5 to 7 minutes or until sausage is no longer pink; drain.

2 Add chicken broth, orzo and bell pepper to sausage in skillet. Heat to boiling over high heat. Reduce heat to low. Cover; cook 10 to 12 minutes or until orzo is tender and liquid is almost evaporated, stirring once during cooking.

3 Stir in Cheddar cheese and cream cheese. Cook and stir over low heat 3 to 4 minutes or until cheese is melted and mixture is thoroughly heated. Garnish with sliced chile.

1 Serving: Calories 610; Total Fat 38g (Saturated Fat 17g, Trans Fat 0.5g); Cholesterol 90mg; Sodium 1260mg; Total Carbohydrate 38g (Dietary Fiber 2g); Protein 27g **Exchanges:** ½ Starch, 2 Other Carbohydrate, ½ Vegetable, 3½ High-Fat Meat, 2 Fat **Carbohydrate Choices:** 2½

Make It a Meal This jalapeño popper–inspired meal is delicious as it is, but if you'd like a bit of extra crunch and color, serve some carrot and celery sticks on the side.

Customize It Some like it hot! If you like spicier food, substitute hot Italian sausage and add an additional jalapeño chile.

American Goulash

Prep Time: 1 Hour • **Start to Finish:** 1 Hour • **6 servings**

1   lb lean (at least 80%) ground beef

1   medium onion, chopped

2   cloves garlic, finely chopped

1½   cups beef broth (from 32-oz carton)

1   can (15 oz) tomato sauce

1   can (14.5 oz) fire-roasted diced tomatoes, undrained

1   tablespoon Italian seasoning

1   teaspoon paprika

¼   teaspoon pepper

1   cup uncooked elbow macaroni (4 oz)

3   oz cream cheese (from 8-oz package), cubed

1   cup shredded Monterey Jack cheese (4 oz)

½   cup flavored croutons, coarsely crushed

1   Heat 12-inch nonstick skillet over medium-high heat. Add beef and onion; cook 5 to 7 minutes, stirring frequently, until beef is thoroughly cooked. Drain; return mixture to skillet.

2   Add garlic to beef in skillet; cook 1 to 2 minutes or until garlic is tender. Stir in broth, tomato sauce, diced tomatoes, Italian seasoning, paprika and pepper. Heat to boiling, stirring occasionally. Reduce heat to low; cover and simmer 18 to 20 minutes or until slightly thickened.

3   Stir in macaroni; cover and cook 16 to 18 minutes, stirring occasionally, until macaroni is tender. Stir in cream cheese; cook until melted, about 3 minutes. Sprinkle with shredded cheese; top with crushed croutons.

1 Serving: Calories 410; Total Fat 20g (Saturated Fat 10g, Trans Fat 1g); Cholesterol 80mg; Sodium 850mg; Total Carbohydrate 33g (Dietary Fiber 3g); Protein 24g **Exchanges:** 1 Starch, 1 Other Carbohydrate, 1 Vegetable, 2 Lean Meat, ½ High-Fat Meat, 2 Fat **Carbohydrate Choices:** 2

Customize It
If you don't have Italian seasoning, substitute 1 teaspoon each of dried basil, dried oregano and dried rosemary in the recipe.

Smothered Beef Burritos

Prep Time: 30 Minutes • Start to Finish: 1 Hour 5 Minutes • 8 burritos

1 tablespoon vegetable oil

1 lb lean (at least 80%) ground beef

1 medium onion chopped (½ cup)

1 package (1 oz) taco seasoning mix

½ cup water

1 package (11 oz) flour tortillas for burritos (8 tortillas, 8 inch)

1 cup refried beans (from 16-oz can)

1½ cups cooked rice

2 cups shredded Mexican cheese blend (8 oz)

1 can (10 oz) enchilada sauce

Chopped fresh cilantro, if desired

Lime wedges, if desired

1 Heat oven to 350°F. In 12-inch ovenproof skillet, heat oil over medium-high heat. Add beef and onion; cook 5 to 7 minutes, stirring frequently, until thoroughly cooked. Drain; return mixture to skillet.

2 Stir taco seasoning mix and water into beef mixture. Cook over medium heat 2 to 3 minutes or until thickened, stirring occasionally. Spoon mixture into medium bowl. Carefully wipe out skillet with paper towel. Spray skillet with cooking spray.

3 Place tortillas on work surface. Divide refried beans, rice and beef mixture in center of each tortilla in 4-inch-long strip. Evenly top with 1 cup of the cheese. Roll up tortillas; place, seam side down, in skillet. Bake uncovered 25 minutes.

4 Drizzle burritos with enchilada sauce; sprinkle with remaining 1 cup cheese. Bake 8 to 10 minutes longer or until cheese is melted and burritos are heated through. Serve with cilantro and lime wedges.

1 Burrito: Calories 430; Total Fat 21g (Saturated Fat 9g, Trans Fat 1.5g); Cholesterol 60mg; Sodium 1070mg; Total Carbohydrate 38g (Dietary Fiber 2g); Protein 22g **Exchanges:** 2 Starch, ½ Other Carbohydrate, 1 Lean Meat, 1 High-Fat Meat, 2 Fat **Carbohydrate Choices:** 2½

Genius Tip To roll burritos, fold 1 edge of tortilla over length of filling, tucking filling in slightly. Then fold 2 short edges over. Roll filled tortilla over toward remaining unfolded edge.

Customize It For a fun twist, swap 1 can of black beans, drained and rinsed, for the refried beans.

Bacon Cheeseburger Meatballs and Gnocchi

Prep Time: 30 Minutes • Start to Finish: 30 Minutes • 6 servings

2 tablespoons butter

1 package (16 oz) shelf-stable gnocchi (not refrigerated or frozen)

½ cup chopped onion

32 frozen beef meatballs (1 inch), thawed (from 22-oz bag)

1 cup beef broth (from 32-oz carton)

1 can (14.5 oz) fire-roasted diced tomatoes, drained

1 cup shredded sharp Cheddar cheese (4 oz)

¾ cup coarsely chopped cooked bacon

2 tablespoons sliced green onions

2 tablespoons chopped dill pickles

1 In 12-inch nonstick skillet, melt 1 tablespoon of the butter over medium-high heat. Add gnocchi; cook 4 to 6 minutes, stirring occasionally, until lightly browned. Spoon gnocchi onto plate; set aside.

2 Reduce heat to medium; melt remaining 1 tablespoon butter in skillet. Add onion and meatballs; cook 4 to 6 minutes, stirring occasionally, until onions are tender and meatballs are thoroughly heated. Add broth, tomatoes and gnocchi to skillet; heat to boiling. Cover; reduce heat to medium-low. Simmer 3 to 5 minutes or until gnocchi are tender. Remove pan from heat.

3 Top gnocchi and meatballs with shredded cheese. Cover; let stand 5 minutes. Just before serving, top with bacon, green onions and pickles.

1 Serving: Calories 410; Total Fat 23g (Saturated Fat 11g, Trans Fat 0.5g); Cholesterol 115mg; Sodium 1160mg; Total Carbohydrate 26g (Dietary Fiber 2g); Protein 25g **Exchanges:** 1½ Starch, 2½ Lean Meat, ½ High Fat Meat, 2 Fat **Carbohydrate Choices:** 2

Genius Tip Potato gnocchi is shelf-stable and can usually be found in the pasta aisle of the grocery store.

Customize It Swapping shredded pepper Jack cheese for the Cheddar cheese transforms this into a spicy cheeseburger skillet.

Tex-Mex Fried Rice

Prep Time: 40 Minutes • Start to Finish: 40 Minutes • 6 servings

FRIED RICE

- 1 lb lean (at least 80%) ground beef
- 1 package (1 oz) taco seasoning mix
- ½ cup water
- ¼ cup vegetable oil
- 1 cup chopped onion
- 1 medium red bell pepper, chopped
- 1 cup frozen whole kernel corn
- ½ teaspoon salt
- 3 cups cooked white rice
- 1 can (4.5 oz) chopped green chiles
- 1 cup shredded Monterey Jack cheese (4 oz)

TOPPINGS, IF DESIRED

Diced avocado

Fresh cilantro

Sliced green onions

Chunky-style salsa

1 In 12-inch nonstick skillet, cook beef over medium-high heat 5 to 7 minutes, stirring frequently, until thoroughly cooked. Drain; return to skillet. Stir in taco seasoning mix and water; heat to simmering over medium heat. Cook 1 to 3 minutes, stirring occasionally, until thickened. Spoon into large bowl; set aside. Carefully wipe out skillet with paper towel.

2 Add oil to skillet; heat over medium-high heat. Add onions, bell pepper, frozen corn and salt. Cook 7 to 10 minutes, stirring frequently, until vegetables are tender and beginning to brown on edges.

3 Add rice and green chiles; cook 4 to 6 minutes, stirring frequently to break up rice, until thoroughly heated. Stir in beef mixture; cook 1 to 2 minutes longer until hot. Remove pan from heat.

4 Sprinkle with cheese. Cover; let stand 1 to 3 minutes or until cheese melts. Top with toppings.

1 Serving: Calories 500; Total Fat 27g (Saturated Fat 10g, Trans Fat 1g); Cholesterol 85mg; Sodium 1040mg; Total Carbohydrate 35g (Dietary Fiber 1g); Protein 27g **Exchanges:** 2 Starch, 1 Vegetable, 2 Lean Meat, ½ High-Fat Meat, 3 Fat **Carbohydrate Choices:** 2

Genius Tip You don't need to cook rice for this recipe. Look for frozen cooked white rice at the grocery store. It is a nice staple to keep in the freezer to help ease the dinner rush on weeknights.

Customize It Make it your own! Try adding Sriracha or chili garlic sauce, experiment with different shredded cheeses, or mix up the diced veggies for your own twist on this easy meal.

Make It Meatless

Love Meatless Mondays? No matter if you're looking to trim your food budget or consume less meat, if you're looking for more ways to go meatless, try these tips below. With these tasty options, you'll never miss it!

These delicious meatless recipes are sprinkled throughout this book. Experiment with the many meatless ways to enjoy dinner:

TRY ONE OF OUR MEATLESS RECIPES

30-Minute Beer Cheese Soup (page 106)

Beans with Spinach and Mushrooms (page 59)

Cheesy Enchilada Rice and Beans (page 259)

Greek-Style Meatless Dinner (page 61)

Impossibly Easy Vegetable Pie (page 310)

Impossibly Easy Ravioli Pie (page 313)

Indian Veggie Couscous (page 62)

Deconstructed Ratatouille (page 162)

Southwest Quinoa-Stuffed Chilies (page 135)

Spicy Tofu and Mushrooms (page 64)

Sweet Potato–Black Bean Lasagna (page 307)

West African Lentil and Vegetable Stew (page 108)

TIPS FOR MAKING DINNERS MEATLESS

- Substitute 2 cups meatless crumbles for recipes that call for 1 pound cooked and drained ground beef. Skip the cooking the beef step, adding the beef crumbles to the recipe where the cooked beef is added with other ingredients. Be sure to heat it through.

- Substitute meatless or vegetarian sausage patties or links for recipes calling for patty or link sausages. Follow directions for cooking on package.

- Substitute 2 cups canned beans such as black beans, garbanzo beans, navy or kidney beans in place of 1 pound cooked ground beef. Rinse and drain canned beans before using.

OTHER WAYS TO GET PROTEIN

"Beef up" your recipes with any of these protein-containing ingredients:

Beans (black beans, garbanzo, kidney, pinto, white, etc.)

Cheese

Edamame (young soybeans before they've ripened or hardened)

Eggs

Lentils

Nuts

Quinoa

Rice and Beans

Seitan (wheat-based meat substitute)

Tempe

Tofu

Whole-grain pastas or rice

MAKING VEGAN DINNERS

If you're looking to make your suppers vegan, try these tips:

- Substitute vegetable broth for the chicken or beef broth. Season the dish with salt after tasting, as vegetable broth can be saltier than the other varieties.

- Substitute milk alternatives (such as cashew or almond) for dairy milk. Read labels as some varieties have more sugar than others, which could change the flavor of a dish.

- Cheese substitutes can give you the sense of eating something rich and creamy, but they don't always replicate the same taste and texture of cheese or melt the way cheese does. Use cheese substitutes in small quantities for best results. Look for them at your local co-op.

- Other foods that can offer a rich and creamy texture and flavor are avocado or hummus. Spread them on sandwiches or on pizzas instead of using cheese.

Taco Supper with Pasta

½ lb lean (at least 80%) ground beef

1 package (1 oz) taco seasoning mix

2¼ cups water

1½ cups uncooked wagon wheel pasta (5½ oz)

1½ cups frozen whole kernel corn

1 can (15 oz) kidney or pinto beans, drained, rinsed

1 medium tomato, chopped (¾ cup)

½ cup sour cream

1 cup shredded Cheddar cheese (4 oz)

1 tablespoon chopped fresh chives

1 In 12-inch skillet, cook beef over medium-high heat 5 to 7 minutes, stirring frequently, until thoroughly cooked; drain.

2 Stir seasoning mix, water, uncooked pasta, corn, beans and tomato into beef. Heat to boiling. Stir; reduce heat to medium-low. Cover; cook 10 to 15 minutes, stirring occasionally, until pasta is desired doneness and most of the liquid has been absorbed.

3 Stir in sour cream. Remove pan from heat. Sprinkle with cheese and chives. Cover; let stand 2 to 3 minutes or until cheese is melted.

1 Serving: Calories 610; Total Fat 24g (Saturated Fat 11g, Trans Fat 1g); Cholesterol 80mg; Sodium 890mg; Total Carbohydrate 68g (Dietary Fiber 8g); Protein 31g **Exchanges:** 1 Starch, 3½ Other Carbohydrate, ½ Vegetable, 3 Medium-Fat Meat, 1 High-Fat Meat **Carbohydrate Choices:** 4½

Customize It Ground turkey can be used in place of the lean ground beef, and fat-free sour cream can be substituted for the regular sour cream.

Make It a Meal Toss mixed greens with shredded carrots and drizzle with your favorite dressing to complete the menu.

Easy Beef Bulgogi

Prep Time: 20 Minutes • Start to Finish: 20 Minutes • 4 servings (1 cup each)

1 lb boneless beef sirloin steak, trimmed of fat

2 tablespoons vegetable oil

1 cup ready-to-eat baby-cut carrots, cut in half lengthwise

3 tablespoons water

2 cups small broccoli florets

1 package (7 oz) Korean stir-fry simmer sauce

4 green onions, cut into 2-inch pieces

1 teaspoon sesame seed

1 cup chopped kimchi (from 14- or 16-oz jar)

1 Cut beef with grain into 2-inch strips; cut strips across grain into ¼-inch strips. In 12-inch nonstick skillet, heat 1 tablespoon of the oil over medium-high heat. Cook beef in oil 3 to 4 minutes, stirring occasionally, until lightly browned. Remove beef from skillet with slotted spoon; keep warm. Discard any liquid in skillet.

2 Add remaining 1 tablespoon oil to skillet; heat 1 minute over medium heat. Add carrots; cook 1 minute, stirring frequently. Add water; cover and cook 2 minutes. Add broccoli; cover and cook 2 minutes more, stirring occasionally, until vegetables are crisp-tender.

3 Add stir-fry simmer sauce, onions and beef. Heat to boiling; reduce heat. Simmer 1 minute or until heated through. Sprinkle with sesame seed. Serve with kimchi.

1 Serving: Calories 320; Total Fat 12g (Saturated Fat 2.5g, Trans Fat 0g); Cholesterol 65mg; Sodium 690mg; Total Carbohydrate 27g (Dietary Fiber 3g); Protein 28g **Exchanges:** 1½ Other Carbohydrate, 1 Vegetable, 3½ Lean Meat, ½ Fat **Carbohydrate Choices:** 2

Find It Short on time? Some grocery stores carry boneless sirloin for stir-fry that is precut for recipes like this Korean-inspired dish.

Genius Tip Bulgogi, which literally means "fire meat," is a popular Korean dish made with thin slices of marinated beef sirloin steak or pork grilled or stir-fried. We've created a quick and easy version served with kimchi, another Korean staple. You could also serve with cooked rice or noodles.

French Onion and Beef Dinner

Prep Time: 30 Minutes • **Start to Finish: 40 Minutes** • **4 servings (1½ cups each)**

1 lb boneless beef
sirloin steak

1¼ teaspoons salt

¼ teaspoon pepper

¼ cup butter

4 cups thinly sliced sweet
onions, cut in half
(about 2 large)

3 tablespoons balsamic
vinegar

2 teaspoons sugar

⅔ cup beef broth (from
32-oz carton)

2 medium red potatoes,
thinly sliced (2 cups)

8 oz Brussels sprouts,
trimmed, cut into
quarters (3 cups)

½ cup shredded
Gruyère cheese

1 Cut beef with grain into 2-inch strips; cut strips across grain into ⅛-inch slices. Sprinkle with ¼ teaspoon of the salt and the pepper.

2 Spray 12-inch nonstick skillet with cooking spray; heat over medium-high heat. Add beef; cook 3 to 4 minutes, stirring frequently, just until beef is browned. Remove skillet from heat. Transfer beef to plate with slotted spoon; cover with foil and keep warm.

3 Add butter and onions to skillet. Cook uncovered 5 minutes, stirring frequently. Stir in vinegar, sugar and the remaining 1 teaspoon salt. Reduce heat to medium. Cook an additional 3 minutes longer, stirring frequently.

4 Stir beef broth and potatoes into onion mixture. Cook covered 8 minutes, stirring occasionally. Stir in Brussels sprouts; cook an additional 5 to 6 minutes longer or until potatoes and Brussels sprouts are tender.

5 Stir in beef; cook until heated. Remove from heat. Sprinkle with cheese; cover and let stand 1 to 2 minutes or until cheese is melted.

1 Serving: Calories 470; Total Fat 20g (Saturated Fat 11g, Trans Fat 0.5g); Cholesterol 110mg; Sodium 1160mg; Total Carbohydrate 38g (Dietary Fiber 6g); Protein 34g **Exchanges:** 2 Starch, 1½ Vegetable, 3 Lean Meat, ½ High-Fat Meat, 1 Fat **Carbohydrate Choices:** 2½

Customize It The rich flavor of Gruyère cheese goes amazingly well in this dish. Or you could substitute Swiss cheese, if that's easier to find.

Genius Tip Cut the meat across the grain? Cutting the meat into strips across the grain helps the cooked meat to be more tender. The grain of the meat is the direction in which the meat fibers are arranged. Slice across the grain, cutting the meat at a 90-degree angle from the meat fibers.

Mapo Tofu with Broccoli

Prep Time: 30 Minutes • Start to Finish: 30 Minutes • 6 servings (1 cup each)

12 oz extra-firm tofu, drained, cut into ½-inch cubes

1¼ cups chicken broth (from 32-oz carton)

2 tablespoons chili garlic sauce

2 tablespoons soy sauce

1 tablespoon vegetable oil

1 lb ground pork

3 cloves garlic, chopped (1 tablespoon)

1 teaspoon grated gingerroot

2 cups frozen baby broccoli florets, thawed (from 12.6-oz bag)

5 teaspoons cornstarch

3 tablespoons water

2 medium green onions, cut diagonally into ½-inch pieces

3 cups cooked white rice

Additional chili garlic sauce, if desired

1 Press tofu cubes between layers of paper towels to remove extra moisture. In small bowl, combine chicken broth, 2 tablespoons chili garlic sauce and the soy sauce; mix well.

2 In 12-inch nonstick skillet, heat oil over medium-high heat. Add tofu; cook 4 to 5 minutes, or until browned on one side. Turn tofu pieces; cook 2 to 4 minutes, stirring occasionally, until browned on all sides. Spoon tofu into medium bowl.

3 Add ground pork to skillet. Cook over medium-high heat 5 to 7 minutes, stirring occasionally, or until no longer pink; drain. Add garlic and gingerroot; cook, stirring constantly 30 seconds. Stir in chicken broth mixture, broccoli and tofu. Heat to boiling.

4 In small bowl, stir cornstarch and water until cornstarch is dissolved. Add cornstarch mixture to skillet. Heat to boiling; reduce heat to low. Simmer uncovered, stirring frequently, 2 to 3 minutes or until sauce thickens and broccoli is crisp-tender. Remove from heat. Sprinkle with green onions. Serve with rice.

1 Serving: Calories 370; Total Fat 17g (Saturated Fat 5g, Trans Fat 0g); Cholesterol 50mg; Sodium 880mg; Total Carbohydrate 31g (Dietary Fiber 2g); Protein 24g **Exchanges:** ½ Starch, 1½ Other Carbohydrate, ½ Vegetable, 3 Very Lean Meat, 3 Fat **Carbohydrate Choices:** 2

Customize It For a meatless meal option, omit the ground pork, increase tofu to 2 packages and use vegetable oil. Or, substitute 1¼ cups frozen meatless crumbles for the ground pork. In step 2, omit cooking and draining the pork. Cook crumbles in skillet, stirring occasionally, until hot. Stir in garlic and ginger; continue as directed.

Genius Tip Mapo Tofu is a popular Chinese dish consisting of tofu cooked in a spicy sauce, usually combined with ground pork or beef and a variety of vegetables.

Sausage and Red Beans with Cornbread Biscuits

Prep Time: 30 Minutes • Start to Finish: 45 Minutes • 6 servings

1   tablespoon butter
1   lb bulk pork sausage
1   cup chopped onion
½   cup chopped celery
½   cup chopped green bell pepper
1   teaspoon Cajun seasoning
⅛   teaspoon ground red pepper (cayenne)
1   can (19 oz) dark red kidney beans, drained, rinsed
1   can (14.5 oz) fire-roasted diced tomatoes, undrained
1   pouch (6.5 oz) cornbread & muffin mix
1   cup shredded sharp Cheddar cheese (4 oz)
2   tablespoons milk
1   tablespoon Sriracha sauce
1   egg
2   green onions, thinly sliced

1 Heat oven to 400°F. In 12-inch ovenproof skillet, melt butter over medium-high heat. Add sausage, onion, celery, bell pepper, Cajun seasoning and red pepper; cook 8 to 10 minutes, stirring occasionally, until sausage is no longer pink and vegetables are tender.

2 Stir in beans and tomatoes. Heat to boiling, stirring frequently. Remove from heat.

3 Meanwhile, in medium bowl, mix cornbread & muffin mix, cheese, milk, Sriracha sauce and egg. Spoon tablespoonfuls over sausage mixture.

4 Bake 12 to 15 minutes or until cornbread biscuits are cooked thoroughly and browned on top. Top with green onions.

1 Serving: Calories 440; Total Fat 20g (Saturated Fat 8g, Trans Fat 0g); Cholesterol 85mg; Sodium 1120mg; Total Carbohydrate 45g (Dietary Fiber 5g); Protein 20g **Exchanges:** 2 Starch, 1 Other Carbohydrate, 2 High-Fat Meat, ½ Fat **Carbohydrate Choices:** 3

Customize It Light red kidney beans can be used instead of the dark variety. Another idea is to use spicy or hot sausage to make the dish.

Pork Chops with Potatoes and Carrots

Prep Time: 10 Minutes • Start to Finish: 50 Minutes • 4 servings

4 pork loin or rib chops,
1 inch thick (1½ lb)

4 medium potatoes, cut
into fourths

4 small carrots, cut into
1-inch pieces

4 medium onions, cut
into fourths

¼ cup beef or chicken broth
(from 32-oz carton)

¾ teaspoon salt

¼ teaspoon pepper

Chopped fresh parsley,
if desired

1 Spray 12-inch skillet with cooking spray; heat over medium-high heat. Cook pork chops in skillet about 5 minutes, turning once, until browned.

2 Add potatoes, carrots, onions and broth to skillet. Sprinkle with salt and pepper. Heat to boiling; reduce heat to low. Cover; simmer 25 to 30 minutes or until vegetables are tender and pork is no longer pink when cut near bone. Sprinkle with parsley.

1 Serving: Calories 500; Total Fat 13g (Saturated Fat 4.5g, Trans Fat 0g); Cholesterol 105mg; Sodium 620mg; Total Carbohydrate 52g (Dietary Fiber 7g); Protein 43g **Exchanges:** 1 Starch, 2 Other Carbohydrate, 2 Vegetable, 5 Very Lean Meat, 2 Fat **Carbohydrate Choices:** 3½

Genius Tip Follow cook times for pork carefully. Today's pork is lean and requires shorter cook times. Overcooking pork will make it tough. Cook just until tender but no longer pink.

Make It a Meal Complete this home-style meal with purchased corn muffins and crisp apple slices drizzled with poppy seed dressing.

Cheesy Ham with Sweet Potatoes

Prep Time: 30 Minutes • Start to Finish: 35 Minutes • 6 servings (1¼ cups each)

2 tablespoons butter

1 lb dark-orange sweet potatoes, peeled, cut into 1-inch cubes

1 small onion, cut into wedges

1 medium red bell pepper, cut lengthwise into ¼-inch strips (1 cup)

2 cloves garlic, finely chopped

2 cups frozen sweet peas

10 oz cooked ham, cut into 1x½x½-inch strips (2 cups)

1 tablespoon all-purpose flour

2 cups half-and-half

¼ teaspoon ground red pepper (cayenne)

4 oz shredded Gruyère or Swiss cheese (1 cup)

2 tablespoons chopped fresh parsley

1 In 12-inch nonstick skillet, melt butter over medium heat. Add sweet potatoes and onion. Cook uncovered, stirring occasionally, 8 to 9 minutes or until sweet potatoes are fork-tender.

2 Stir in bell pepper, garlic, peas and ham; cook 30 seconds. Stir in flour until well mixed. Slowly add half-and-half and red pepper.

3 Cook uncovered, stirring frequently, 4 to 5 minutes or until slightly thickened. Reduce heat to medium-low; sprinkle with cheese. Cook uncovered, stirring occasionally, 1 to 2 minutes or until cheese is melted and mixture is thoroughly heated. Let stand 5 minutes before serving. Garnish with parsley leaves.

1 Serving: Calories 420; Total Fat 23g (Saturated Fat 13g, Trans Fat 0.5g); Cholesterol 85mg; Sodium 970mg; Total Carbohydrate 30g (Dietary Fiber 5g); Protein 23g **Exchanges:** 1 Starch, ½ Other Carbohydrate, 1 Vegetable, 2 Very Lean Meat, ½ High-Fat Meat, 3½ Fat **Carbohydrate Choices:** 2

Customize It Switch up the meat in this dish by using chopped cooked chicken or Canadian bacon strips for the ham.

Genius Tip Sweet potatoes are a root vegetable frequently mislabeled as yams. They are available in colors ranging from white to red. We prefer dark orange sweet potatoes in this recipe for the sweetness and color they add to the dish.

BBQ Hot Dogs with Potatoes

Prep Time: 20 Minutes • Start to Finish: 30 Minutes • 6 servings (1 cup each)

1 package (12 oz) beef hot dogs, cut in half lengthwise then cut into 1-inch pieces

2 tablespoons vegetable oil

1 package (20 oz) refrigerated diced potatoes

½ cup chopped onion

½ teaspoon salt

¼ teaspoon pepper

1 package (10.8 oz) frozen lightly seasoned southwestern corn, thawed

1 cup shredded Cheddar cheese

⅓ cup barbecue sauce

Sliced green onion or chopped cilantro, if desired

1 In 12-inch nonstick skillet, place hot dogs; cook over medium-high heat about 5 minutes, stirring occasionally, until browned. Spoon hot dogs into small bowl; cover.

2 In same skillet, heat oil over medium heat. Add potatoes and onion in single layer; sprinkle with salt and pepper. Cover; cook 10 to 12 minutes, stirring every 3 to 4 minutes, until potatoes are browned. Add corn and hot dogs to skillet; cook and stir 2 to 3 minutes, or until thoroughly heated.

3 Sprinkle with cheese. Cover; cook 1 to 2 minutes, or until cheese is melted. Drizzle with barbecue sauce; garnish with green onion.

1 Serving: Calories 450; Total Fat 28g (Saturated Fat 11g, Trans Fat 1g); Cholesterol 50mg; Sodium 1190mg; Total Carbohydrate 34g (Dietary Fiber 3g); Protein 14g **Exchanges:** 1 Starch, 1½ Other Carbohydrate, 1½ High-Fat Meat, 3 Fat **Carbohydrate Choices:** 2

Genius Tip Miniature cocktail wieners are a fun and kid-friendly substitute for regular hot dogs in this recipe.

Customize It Instead of barbecue sauce, use your favorite variety of ketchup. Or substitute regular sweet corn in place of the southwestern corn.

Sesame Shrimp Stir-Fry

Prep Time: 30 Minutes • Start to Finish: 30 Minutes • 4 servings

RICE

- 2 cups chicken broth (from 32-oz carton)
- 1 cup uncooked jasmine rice
- 1/4 teaspoon salt

SHRIMP AND VEGETABLES

- 1/3 cup Asian sesame dressing (from 8-oz bottle)
- 1/3 cup water
- 1 tablespoon cornstarch
- 1 tablespoon soy sauce
- 1 tablespoon chili garlic sauce
- 1 tablespoon vegetable oil
- 1 bag (12 oz) fresh stir-fry vegetables
- 1 lb uncooked deveined peeled large shrimp, tail shells removed, thawed if frozen
- 1 teaspoon roasted sesame seed

1 In large microwavable bowl, mix broth, rice and salt. Cover with plastic wrap; microwave on High 5 minutes; stir. Microwave on Medium (50%) 15 minutes. Let stand covered 5 minutes. Carefully uncover; stir. Keep warm.

2 In small bowl, mix dressing, water, cornstarch, soy sauce and chili garlic sauce; beat with fork until smooth. Set aside.

3 In 12-inch skillet, heat oil over medium-high heat. Add vegetables; cook 2 minutes, stirring constantly. Add shrimp; cook 4 to 6 minutes, stirring frequently, until shrimp turn pink and vegetables are crisp-tender.

4 Stir dressing mixture into shrimp mixture; heat to boiling. Cook and stir 1 to 2 minutes or until sauce is thickened. Sprinkle with sesame seed. Serve with rice.

1 Serving: Calories 430; Total Fat 12g (Saturated Fat 1.5g, Trans Fat 0g); Cholesterol 155mg; Sodium 1190mg; Total Carbohydrate 52g (Dietary Fiber 2g); Protein 26g **Exchanges:** 1½ Starch, 1½ Other Carbohydrate, 1 Vegetable, 3 Lean Meat, ½ Fat **Carbohydrate Choices:** 3½

Genius Tip Fresh and frozen shrimp are sold by a descriptive size name like jumbo or large, and by "count," or number per pound. The larger the shrimp, the lower the count. Size and count vary throughout the United States.

Customize It Roasted sesame seed can be found in the Asian section of most grocery stores. If you can't find it, plain white sesame seed makes a fine substitute.

Lemon-Basil Orzo and Vegetables

Prep Time: 20 Minutes • Start to Finish: 35 Minutes • 5 servings (about 1½ cups each)

3 tablespoons olive oil

2 medium zucchini, cut into ¼-inch slices

1 medium onion, chopped

2 cloves garlic, finely chopped

8 oz uncooked orzo or rosamarina pasta (1 cup)

1½ cups vegetable broth (from 32-oz carton)

1 can (14.5 oz) fire-roasted diced tomatoes, undrained

1 can (19 oz) chick peas (garbanzo beans), drained, rinsed

2 teaspoons grated lemon peel

½ teaspoon salt

¼ teaspoon pepper

1 tablespoon lemon juice

¼ cup julienne-cut fresh basil leaves

1 In 12-inch nonstick skillet, heat 1 tablespoon oil over medium-high heat. Add zucchini; cook 2 to 3 minutes, stirring occasionally, until zucchini is light brown. Spoon zucchini onto plate.

2 Add remaining 2 tablespoons oil, the onion and garlic to skillet. Cook and stir 2 to 3 minutes or until tender. Add orzo; cook and stir 2 to 3 minutes or until orzo is lightly toasted. Stir in broth, tomatoes, chick peas, lemon peel, salt and pepper. Heat to boiling; cover, and reduce heat to low. Cook 8 to 10 minutes or until most of liquid has absorbed and orzo is almost tender.

3 Add zucchini and lemon juice to orzo mixture; stir to combine. Remove from heat. Cover; let stand 3 to 5 minutes or until all the liquid is absorbed. Stir in basil.

1 Serving: Calories 410; Total Fat 11g (Saturated Fat 1.5g, Trans Fat 0g); Cholesterol 0mg; Sodium 630mg; Total Carbohydrate 63g (Dietary Fiber 8g); Protein 14g **Exchanges:** 1 Starch, 2½ Other Carbohydrate, 2 Vegetable, 1 Very Lean Meat, 2 Fat **Carbohydrate Choices:** 4

Customize It For added richness and flavor, drizzle a little olive oil over the finished dish.

Genius Tip Cooking lemon juice dulls the flavor. For that reason, we add the lemon peel early in the cooking process but save the juice for the end so the lively lemon flavor is preserved.

Beans with Spinach and Mushrooms

Prep Time: 15 Minutes • Start to Finish: 25 Minutes • 4 servings (1¾ cups each)

2 tablespoons olive oil

1 package (8 oz) sliced fresh mushrooms (3 cups)

1 medium onion, chopped (½ cup)

2 cloves garlic, finely chopped

¾ teaspoon dried oregano leaves

½ cup vegetable broth (from 32-oz carton)

1 tablespoon cornstarch

1 can (15.8 oz) great northern beans, drained, rinsed

1 can (15.5 oz) chick peas (garbanzo beans), drained, rinsed

1 can (14.5 oz) diced tomatoes with basil, garlic and oregano, undrained

4 cups coarsely chopped spinach or baby spinach leaves (about 5 oz)

¼ cup shredded Parmesan cheese

1 In 12-inch skillet, heat oil over medium-high heat. Add mushrooms, onion, garlic and oregano; cook 3 to 5 minutes, stirring frequently, until mushrooms are tender.

2 In small bowl, stir together vegetable broth and cornstarch.

3 Stir beans, tomatoes and vegetable broth mixture into mushrooms in skillet. Heat to boiling; cook 1 minute or until mixture is thickened and bubbly. Gradually stir in spinach. Cook 1 to 2 minutes or until wilted. Sprinkle with cheese.

1 Serving: Calories 370; Total Fat 11g (Saturated Fat 2.5g, Trans Fat 0g); Cholesterol 0mg; Sodium 750mg; Total Carbohydrate 48g (Dietary Fiber 12g); Protein 18g **Exchanges:** 1 Starch, 2 Other Carbohydrate, 1 Vegetable, 2 Very Lean Meat, 2 Fat **Carbohydrate Choices:** 3

Customize It
If you like, you can substitute baby kale, chopped turnip, mustard or beet greens for the spinach leaves. You may need to cook them a minute or two longer for them to wilt.

Genius Tip
Why rinse your canned beans? Sometimes it's not necessary to rinse beans, especially when you are making a stew or chili and you want to thicken the mixture. But for salads, sautés and sandwiches, rinsing and draining the canned beans removes the liquid the beans are processed in, which contains starch and sodium and can give the dish a cloudy appearance.

Greek-Style Meatless Dinner

Prep Time: 25 Minutes • Start to Finish: 25 Minutes • 4 servings (1 cup each)

1 tablespoon olive oil

1 clove garlic, finely chopped

2 cups frozen meatless crumbles (from 16.2-oz package)

1 can (14.5 oz) diced tomatoes, undrained

1 cup water

2 teaspoons Greek seasoning

½ cup uncooked orzo or rosamarina pasta

1 can (15.5 oz) chick peas (garbanzo beans), drained, rinsed

2 cups packed fresh baby spinach leaves (from 6-oz bag)

½ cup crumbled feta cheese

2 tablespoons chopped red onion

2 tablespoons chopped fresh Italian (flat-leaf) parsley

1 In 12-inch nonstick skillet, heat oil over medium heat. Add garlic; cook 1 minute, stirring constantly.

2 Add meatless crumbles, tomatoes, water and Greek seasoning; heat to boiling. Stir in orzo and chick peas. Heat to boiling; reduce heat to low. Cover; simmer 14 to 17 minutes, stirring once, until orzo is tender.

3 Add spinach; cook 2 to 3 minutes, stirring occasionally, until spinach is wilted. Remove from heat. Top with cheese, red onion and parsley.

1 Serving: Calories 360; Total Fat 10g (Saturated Fat 3.5g, Trans Fat 0g); Cholesterol 15mg; Sodium 1240mg; Total Carbohydrate 42g (Dietary Fiber 9g); Protein 24g **Exchanges:** 1½ Starch, 1 Other Carbohydrate, 1 Vegetable, 2 Very Lean Meat, ½ Medium-Fat Meat, 1 Fat **Carbohydrate Choices:** 3

Make It a Meal Top each serving with a dollop of tzatziki cucumber sauce (usually found near the refrigerated deli items at your supermarket). You can also serve with pita bread, cut into wedges.

Customize It Try using baby kale in place of the spinach. Baby kale is more delicate than mature kale and will add a slight peppery flavor to the dish.

Genius Tip If you need a substitute for the Greek seasoning, just use ½ teaspoon dried oregano leaves, ½ teaspoon dried thyme leaves, ½ teaspoon dried basil leaves and ½ teaspoon salt.

Indian Veggie Couscous

Prep Time: 15 Minutes • Start to Finish: 30 Minutes • 4 servings (1¼ cups each)

2 cups vegetable broth (from 32-oz carton)

2 tablespoons plus 2 teaspoons butter

1 box (10 oz) Mediterranean curry couscous

1½ cups cubed butternut squash (7 oz)

1 medium red bell pepper, coarsely chopped (1 cup)

2 cloves garlic, finely chopped

1 cup frozen whole kernel corn

1 cup frozen shelled edamame (green soybeans)

½ teaspoon garam masala

Dash ground red pepper (cayenne)

1 In 12-inch nonstick skillet, mix 1¼ cups of the vegetable broth, 2 teaspoons of the butter and the seasoning packet from couscous; heat to boiling. Stir in couscous. Cover; remove from heat. Let stand 5 minutes. Spoon couscous into medium bowl; cover to keep warm.

2 In same skillet, melt remaining 2 tablespoons butter over medium heat. Add squash, bell pepper and garlic; cook uncovered, stirring occasionally, 8 to 10 minutes or until squash is fork-tender.

3 Stir in remaining ¾ cup broth, the corn, edamame, garam masala and ground red pepper. Cook uncovered, stirring occasionally, 4 to 5 minutes or until thoroughly heated. Stir in couscous.

1 Serving: Calories 430; Total Fat 11g (Saturated Fat 5g, Trans Fat 0g); Cholesterol 20mg; Sodium 1010mg; Total Carbohydrate 67g (Dietary Fiber 8g); Protein 15g **Exchanges:** 2 Starch, 2 Other Carbohydrate, 1 Vegetable, 1 Very Lean Meat, 2 Fat **Carbohydrate Choices:** 4½

Customize It To scoop up every bit of this deliciousness, serve the couscous with warm pita bread or naan.

Find It Couscous is tiny pasta that cooks very quickly, making it perfect for easy meals. You can find couscous in the rice aisle of your favorite grocery store.

Genius Tip For quicker preparation, look for peeled, cut-up butternut squash in the produce aisle of your favorite grocery store.

Spicy Tofu and Mushrooms

Prep Time: 15 Minutes • Start to Finish: 45 Minutes • 4 servings (1¼ cups each)

1 package (9 oz) extra-firm tofu, drained, cut into 1-inch cubes

⅓ cup hoisin sauce

2 tablespoons soy sauce

2 cloves garlic, finely chopped

2 teaspoons finely chopped gingerroot

1 teaspoon sugar

¼ teaspoon crushed red pepper flakes

¼ teaspoon salt, if desired

1 tablespoon sesame oil

1 package (12 oz) fresh green beans (about 3 cups)

1 package (8 oz) baby portabella mushrooms, quartered

2 teaspoons sesame seed, if desired

1 tablespoon chopped fresh cilantro, if desired

1 Pat tofu dry with paper towels. In medium bowl, beat hoisin sauce, soy sauce, garlic, gingerroot, sugar, red pepper flakes and salt with whisk until well blended. Add tofu, toss to coat. Let stand 30 minutes.

2 In 12-inch nonstick skillet, heat sesame oil over medium heat. Add green beans and mushrooms. Cook, stirring occasionally, 8 to 10 minutes or until green beans are crisp-tender.

3 Add tofu mixture; cook, stirring occasionally, 3 to 4 minutes or until thoroughly heated. Sprinkle with sesame seed and cilantro.

1 Serving: Calories 200; Total Fat 8g (Saturated Fat 1.5g, Trans Fat 0g); Cholesterol 0mg; Sodium 800mg; Total Carbohydrate 20g (Dietary Fiber 4g); Protein 10g **Exchanges:** 1 Other Carbohydrate, 1½ Vegetable, 1 Very Lean Meat, 1½ Fat **Carbohydrate Choices:** 1

Make It a Meal
Add a side of cooked brown or jasmine rice when you serve this delicious dish.

Genius Tip
Extra-firm tofu works best for stir-frying as it cuts easily and doesn't fall apart during cooking. Look for tofu in the refrigerated section of the produce area of your grocery store.

Big Pot

Carbonara Chicken with Gnocchi

Prep Time: 25 Minutes • Start to Finish: 25 Minutes • 4 servings

5 slices bacon, cut into ½-inch pieces

2 cloves garlic, finely chopped

¾ cup milk

2 cups shredded cooked chicken

1 jar (15 oz) Alfredo pasta sauce

1 package (16 oz) shelf-stable gnocchi (not refrigerated or frozen)

¼ teaspoon red pepper flakes

3 cups packed fresh baby spinach leaves (from 6-oz bag)

¼ cup freshly shredded Parmesan cheese

1 In 5-quart Dutch oven or 4-quart saucepan, cook bacon over medium-high heat until crisp. Using slotted spoon, remove bacon to paper towel–lined plate; set aside. Reserve 1 tablespoon bacon drippings in pan.

2 Add garlic to bacon drippings; cook over medium heat 1 minute, stirring constantly. Stir in milk, chicken, Alfredo sauce, gnocchi and red pepper flakes. Heat to boiling, stirring frequently; reduce heat. Simmer uncovered 3 to 5 minutes, stirring constantly, until gnocchi is tender.

3 Stir in spinach and bacon; cook until spinach is wilted, about 1 minute. Sprinkle with Parmesan cheese.

1 Serving: Calories 750; Total Fat 45g (Saturated Fat 25g, Trans Fat 1.5g); Cholesterol 175mg; Sodium 1230mg; Total Carbohydrate 51g (Dietary Fiber 2g); Protein 37g **Exchanges:** 3 Starch, ½ Vegetable, 3 Very Lean Meat, ½ Lean Meat, 8 Fat **Carbohydrate Choices:** 3½

Genius Tip Gnocchi is actually a type of Italian pasta that is small with a dumpling-like shape and texture. It is generally made with cooked potatoes, flour and egg.

Find It Gnocchi is available as a shelf-stable, refrigerated or frozen product. This recipe uses the shelf-stable product found with the dry pastas in your grocery store. The shelf-stable product is actually vacuum-packed and not dried, making any recipe using it extra quick to prepare!

Buffalo Chicken Penne Pasta

Prep Time: 20 Minutes • Start to Finish: 45 Minutes • 5 servings (1⅓ cups each)

2 stalks celery, chopped (⅔ cup)

1 tablespoon vegetable oil

1 package (10 oz) fully-cooked chicken bratwurst or sausage, cut into ½-inch slices

1 medium onion, chopped (½ cup)

1 container (32 oz) reduced-sodium chicken broth

⅓ cup buffalo wing sauce

8 oz uncooked penne pasta (2½ cups)

¾ cup frozen sweet peas

4 oz cream cheese, cubed

½ cup shredded Monterey Jack cheese (2 oz)

⅓ cup crumbled blue cheese

2 medium green onions, thinly sliced

1 Reserve 2 tablespoons chopped celery; set aside. In 5-quart Dutch oven, heat oil over medium-high heat; add chicken bratwurst, onion and remaining celery. Cook 4 to 6 minutes, stirring occasionally, until bratwurst is browned and vegetables are tender. Spoon bratwurst mixture into medium bowl.

2 Add chicken broth, buffalo wing sauce and pasta to Dutch oven. Heat to boiling; reduce heat. Simmer uncovered 13 to 15 minutes, stirring frequently, until pasta is tender and most of the liquid is absorbed.

3 Add peas, cream cheese and Monterey Jack cheese, stirring constantly, until cheese is melted. Add bratwurst mixture back to Dutch oven, stirring frequently, until thoroughly heated. Top with reserved celery, blue cheese and green onions.

1 Serving: Calories 530; Total Fat 26g (Saturated Fat 11g, Trans Fat 0.5g); Cholesterol 70mg; Sodium 1260mg; Total Carbohydrate 48g (Dietary Fiber 4g); Protein 26g **Exchanges:** 2 Starch, 1 Other Carbohydrate, ½ Vegetable, 2 Lean Meat, ½ Medium-Fat Meat, 3½ Fat **Carbohydrate Choices:** 3

Customize It For a change of flavor, substitute the blue cheese with feta cheese or use additional shredded Monterey Jack cheese in place of the blue cheese.

Customize It Fully-cooked chicken sausage and bratwurst are available in many varieties. Choose your favorite variety for this recipe.

Sesame Chicken and Noodles

Prep Time: 40 Minutes • Start to Finish: 40 Minutes • 6 servings

6 boneless skinless chicken thighs (1¼ lb), cut into ½-inch strips

12 oz uncooked spaghetti, broken in half

1 medium red bell pepper, cut in thin strips

3 green onions, thinly sliced, white and green parts separated

1 package (3½ oz) shiitake mushrooms, stems removed, thinly sliced

1 carton (32 oz) chicken broth

¼ cup butter

2 tablespoons hoisin sauce

1 tablespoon toasted sesame oil

1 tablespoon soy sauce

2 teaspoons chili garlic sauce

2 tablespoons chopped fresh cilantro

1 tablespoon sesame seed

1 In 5-quart Dutch oven, mix chicken, spaghetti, bell pepper, green onion whites, mushrooms, broth, butter, hoisin sauce, sesame oil, soy sauce and chili garlic sauce. Heat to boiling over high heat, stirring occasionally.

2 Reduce heat to medium-low; cook 11 to 15 minutes, stirring occasionally, until juice of chicken is clear when thickest part is cut (at least 165°F), pasta is cooked and most of liquid is absorbed. Top with green onion greens, cilantro and sesame seed.

1 Serving: Calories 500; Total Fat 17g (Saturated Fat 7g, Trans Fat 0g); Cholesterol 110mg; Sodium 960mg; Total Carbohydrate 55g (Dietary Fiber 4g); Protein 31g **Exchanges:** 2½ Starch, 1 Other Carbohydrate, ½ Vegetable, 3 Very Lean Meat, 3 Fat **Carbohydrate Choices:** 3½

Customize It Shiitake mushrooms are delicious, but you could substitute button mushrooms if you like.

Genius Tip Stir, stir, stir! One-pot pastas cook quickly, so don't forget to stir often to prevent noodles from sticking.

Creamy Chicken Pot Pie Pasta

Prep Time: 30 Minutes • **Start to Finish: 30 Minutes** • **6 servings**

4¼ cups uncooked wide egg noodles (8 oz)

2 cups shredded cooked chicken

2 cups frozen mixed vegetables

1 carton (32 oz) chicken broth

1 teaspoon dried thyme leaves

½ teaspoon salt

½ teaspoon pepper

½ cup half-and-half

2 tablespoons chopped Italian (flat-leaf) parsley, if desired

1 In 5-quart Dutch oven, mix egg noodles, chicken, mixed vegetables, broth, thyme, salt and pepper (ingredients will be above liquid). Heat to boiling. Reduce heat to medium; cook uncovered 8 to 10 minutes, stirring occasionally, until most of liquid is absorbed and pasta is tender.

2 Stir in half-and-half; cook 1 to 2 minutes or until thoroughly heated. Top with parsley.

1 Serving: Calories 260; Total Fat 8g (Saturated Fat 3g, Trans Fat 0g); Cholesterol 75mg; Sodium 800mg; Total Carbohydrate 28g (Dietary Fiber 2g); Protein 19g **Exchanges:** 1 Starch, ½ Other Carbohydrate, ½ Vegetable, 2 Very Lean Meat, 1½ Fat **Carbohydrate Choices:** 2

Genius Tip Rotisserie chicken is great to use for shredded cooked chicken.

Make It a Meal Serve with a side of crusty bread and a fresh green salad.

Cheesy Chicken and Sausage

Prep Time: 40 Minutes • Start to Finish: 40 Minutes • 6 servings (1⅓ cups each)

2 tablespoons olive oil

½ lb fresh chorizo or bulk pork sausage

1¼ lb boneless skinless chicken thighs, cut into 1-inch pieces

1 large onion, chopped (1 cup)

½ teaspoon salt

1 tablespoon taco seasoning mix (from 1-oz package)

1 can (4.5 oz) chopped green chiles

1 can (28 oz) whole tomatoes, undrained

1 can (15 oz) black beans, drained, rinsed

2 cups shredded Monterey Jack or pepper Jack cheese (8 oz)

4½ cups hot cooked rice or 6 flour tortillas (6 inch), heated as directed on package, if desired

2 cups coarsely crushed tortilla chips

¼ cup chopped fresh cilantro

6 lime wedges

1 In 5-quart Dutch oven, heat 1 tablespoon of the oil over medium heat. Add sausage; cook 6 to 10 minutes, stirring occasionally, until no longer pink. Drain. Spoon sausage onto plate; set aside.

2 Add chicken to Dutch oven; cook 6 to 10 minutes, stirring occasionally, until no longer pink in center. Spoon onto plate with sausage.

3 Add remaining 1 tablespoon oil to Dutch oven. Add onion and salt. Cook 4 to 5 minutes or until onion is softened. Stir in taco seasoning mix and chiles; cook 1 minute. Add tomatoes. Heat to boiling. Stir in sausage, chicken and beans. Reduce heat to medium; cook 5 minutes, stirring occasionally until flavors are blended. Stir in cheese.

4 Serve mixture over rice or spoon into tortillas. Top with chips and cilantro. Serve with lime wedges.

1 Serving: Calories 730; Total Fat 42g (Saturated Fat 16g, Trans Fat 0g); Cholesterol 130mg; Sodium 1460mg; Total Carbohydrate 42g (Dietary Fiber 8g); Protein 46g **Exchanges:** 1½ Starch, 1 Other Carbohydrate, 1 Vegetable, 3 Lean Meat, 2½ High-Fat Meat, 2½ Fat **Carbohydrate Choices:** 3

Genius Tip If you are wondering what to do with leftover taco seasoning, here are some ideas. Stir it into softened butter and brush on corn on the cob before grilling, stir into sour cream for a zippy dip or mix into an oil-and-vinegar dressing for a south-of-the-border twist.

Lemon-Pepper Chicken Pasta

Prep Time: 45 Minutes • Start to Finish: 50 Minutes • 6 servings

1 lb boneless skinless chicken breasts, cut into bite-size pieces

1 teaspoon lemon-pepper seasoning

½ teaspoon salt

¼ teaspoon black pepper

1 tablespoon olive oil

1 tablespoon finely chopped garlic

1 carton (32 oz) chicken broth

8 oz uncooked spaghetti, broken in half

½ cup shredded Parmesan cheese (2 oz)

2 tablespoons butter

1 tablespoon lemon juice

2 teaspoons grated lemon peel

2 bags (5 oz each) baby spinach

1 Sprinkle chicken with lemon-pepper seasoning, salt and black pepper. In 5-quart Dutch oven, heat oil over medium-high heat. Add chicken; cook 5 to 7 minutes, stirring occasionally, until chicken is no longer pink. Place chicken on plate; cover to keep warm.

2 Add garlic to Dutch oven; cook 30 to 60 seconds, stirring constantly, until lightly browned. Add chicken broth and spaghetti; heat to boiling. Reduce heat to medium; cook uncovered 13 to 15 minutes, stirring occasionally, until most of liquid is absorbed and pasta is al dente.

3 Stir in ¼ cup of the Parmesan cheese, the butter, lemon juice, lemon peel and cooked chicken. Remove from heat. Gradually add spinach; stir just until starting to wilt. Let stand 5 minutes before serving. Serve warm with remaining ¼ cup shredded Parmesan cheese.

1 Serving: Calories 370; Total Fat 12g (Saturated Fat 5g, Trans Fat 0g); Cholesterol 65mg; Sodium 1040mg; Total Carbohydrate 37g (Dietary Fiber 3g); Protein 28g **Exchanges:** 2 Starch, ½ Other Carbohydrate, 3 Lean Meat, ½ Fat **Carbohydrate Choices:** 2½

Genius Tip Due to the bulkiness of the spinach, it's helpful to add it to pasta in small batches. But watch carefully as it wilts quickly!

Customize It If you prefer more peppery flavor, increase black pepper from ¼ teaspoon to ½ teaspoon.

Swedish Meatballs with Egg Noodles

Prep Time: 50 Minutes • Start to Finish: 50 Minutes • 6 servings

1 lb lean (at least 80%) ground beef

1 cup plain panko crispy bread crumbs

½ cup finely chopped onion

¼ cup finely chopped fresh Italian (flat-leaf) parsley

2 teaspoons salt

½ teaspoon pepper

¼ teaspoon ground allspice

⅓ cup milk

1 teaspoon Worcestershire sauce

1 egg

1 tablespoon butter

1 carton (32 oz) chicken broth

¾ cup whipping cream

4 cups uncooked medium egg noodles (about 8 oz)

1 In large bowl, mix beef, bread crumbs, onion, 2 tablespoons of the parsley, 1 teaspoon of the salt, the pepper and allspice until well combined. Add milk, Worcestershire sauce and egg. Shape mixture into 12 (2-inch) meatballs.

2 In 5-quart Dutch oven, melt butter over medium-high heat. Add meatballs; cook 8 to 11 minutes, gently turning occasionally, just until browned on all sides.

3 Add broth, whipping cream and remaining 1 teaspoon salt; heat to boiling. Stir in noodles; return to boiling. Reduce heat; simmer uncovered 15 to 18 minutes, stirring occasionally, until meatballs are thoroughly cooked and no longer pink in center, pasta is cooked and sauce is thickened. Stir in remaining 2 tablespoons parsley.

1 Serving: Calories 450; Total Fat 25g (Saturated Fat 12g, Trans Fat 1g); Cholesterol 145mg; Sodium 1460mg; Total Carbohydrate 36g (Dietary Fiber 1g); Protein 21g **Exchanges:** 2 Starch, ½ Other Carbohydrate, 1 Lean Meat, 1 Medium-Fat Meat, 3 Fat **Carbohydrate Choices:** 2½

Make It a Meal For extra Swedish flair, serve with lingonberry jam.

Genius Tip This easy one-pot cooks quickly, so don't forget to stir often to prevent the noodles from sticking.

Curry Meatball Soup

Prep Time: 20 Minutes • Start to Finish: 35 Minutes • 6 servings (1⅓ cups each)

1 lb frozen cooked meatballs (from 22-oz bag)

1 large onion, chopped (about 1 cup)

2 cups chicken broth (from 32-oz carton)

1 can (14.5 oz) diced tomatoes with green chiles, undrained

1 package (10.8 oz) frozen broccoli, carrots, sugar snap peas and water chestnuts

2 teaspoons curry powder

½ teaspoon salt

1 can (13.66 oz) unsweetened coconut milk (not cream of coconut)

1 tablespoon chopped fresh cilantro

1 In 4-quart saucepan, cook meatballs and onion over medium heat 5 to 6 minutes or until meatballs are brown and onion is tender. Add chicken broth, tomatoes, frozen vegetables, curry powder and salt.

2 Heat to boiling. Cover; reduce heat to low. Simmer 8 to 10 minutes or until carrots are crisp-tender. Stir in coconut milk and cilantro. Cook until thoroughly heated, stirring occasionally.

1 Serving: Calories 350; Total Fat 21g (Saturated Fat 14g, Trans Fat 0g); Cholesterol 75mg; Sodium 1070mg; Total Carbohydrate 21g (Dietary Fiber 3g); Protein 18g **Exchanges:** 1 Starch, ½ Vegetable, 2 Medium-Fat Meat, 2 Fat **Carbohydrate Choices:** 1½

Customize It The recipe calls for frozen cooked meatballs so you can choose any of your favorite cooked meatballs, such as beef, chicken, sausage or turkey. Smaller, bite-size meatballs are great for easy eating.

Genius Tip If you can't find vegetable mixture listed, you can substitute a 10.8-bag of lightly sauced Asian frozen vegetables or your favorite frozen vegetable mix instead.

Find It Look for unsweetened coconut milk in the global food aisle of the grocery store next to Asian and Indian foods.

Beef Stroganoff

Prep Time: 45 Minutes • Start to Finish: 50 Minutes • 6 servings

1¼ lb boneless beef sirloin steak, cut into thin strips

1 tablespoon Montreal steak seasoning

4 tablespoons butter

1 package (8 oz) mushrooms, thinly sliced

½ cup finely chopped onion

1 carton (32 oz) beef broth

½ cup sour cream

4 cups uncooked medium egg noodles (about 8 oz)

Finely chopped fresh Italian (flat-leaf) parsley, if desired

1 In medium bowl, mix beef and steak seasoning. In 5-quart Dutch oven, melt 2 tablespoons of the butter over medium-high heat. Add steak in single layer; cook 4 to 7 minutes, turning once, just until browned on both sides. Using tongs, transfer beef to plate; cover with foil to keep warm.

2 Add remaining 2 tablespoons butter to drippings in Dutch oven; melt over medium-high heat. Add mushrooms and onion. Cook 7 to 9 minutes, stirring frequently, until mushrooms brown and onion is tender.

3 Stir in broth; heat to boiling. Place sour cream in medium bowl. Using ladle, spoon ½ cup hot liquid into sour cream; beat with whisk to combine. Set aside.

4 Stir noodles into mixture in Dutch oven; heat to boiling. Reduce heat; simmer uncovered 10 to 15 minutes, stirring occasionally, until noodles are tender and most of liquid is reduced (mixture will be saucy). Stir in beef and any accumulated liquid; return to boiling. Remove from heat; stir in sour cream mixture. Let stand 5 minutes before serving. Sprinkle with parsley.

1 Serving: Calories 380; Total Fat 17g (Saturated Fat 9g, Trans Fat 0.5g); Cholesterol 110mg; Sodium 1060mg; Total Carbohydrate 30g (Dietary Fiber 2g); Protein 27g **Exchanges:** 1 Starch, ½ Other Carbohydrate, 1 Vegetable, 3 Lean Meat, 1½ Fat **Carbohydrate Choices:** 2

Genius Tip For better browning, pat beef dry before tossing with steak seasoning, and make sure butter is quite hot before adding steak to Dutch oven.

Make It a Meal Serve this classic dish with buttered broccoli spears and crispy French bread slices.

Pork Marbella Stew

Prep Time: 20 Minutes • Start to Finish: 4 Hours 20 Minutes • 4 servings (1½ cups each)

1½ lb pork tenderloin, cut into 1-inch cubes

4 cloves garlic, finely chopped

¼ cup olive oil

¼ cup balsamic vinegar

1 tablespoon chopped fresh oregano leaves or 1 teaspoon dried oregano leaves

1 teaspoon salt

¼ teaspoon pepper

½ cup pitted prunes

1 lb baby white creamer potatoes, halved (from 1.5-oz package)

¼ cup packed brown sugar

2 tablespoons all-purpose flour

1 cup beef broth (from 32-oz carton)

1 medium red bell pepper, chopped (1 cup)

½ cup pimiento-stuffed olives

2 tablespoons capers

1 In 2-gallon resealable food-storage plastic bag, combine pork tenderloin, garlic, oil, vinegar, oregano, salt, pepper and prunes. Shake to coat. Refrigerate 3 to 4 hours to marinate.

2 Heat oven to 350°F. In 5- to 6-quart ovenproof Dutch oven, mix pork mixture, potatoes and brown sugar.

3 Bake covered 40 minutes. Remove from oven. Stir in flour. Slowly stir in broth until well mixed. Stir in bell pepper, olives and capers.

4 Bake uncovered 15 to 20 minutes longer or until slightly thickened and potatoes are tender.

1 Serving: Calories 600; Total Fat 24g (Saturated Fat 5g, Trans Fat 0g); Cholesterol 105mg; Sodium 1300mg; Total Carbohydrate 54g (Dietary Fiber 5g); Protein 42g **Exchanges:** 1½ Starch, 2 Other Carbohydrate, ½ Vegetable, 5 Very Lean Meat, 4 Fat **Carbohydrate Choices:** 3½

Customize It Traditional Marbella is prepared with a whole, cut-up chicken. This new version is made with a pork twist. If you like chicken, use chicken thighs in place of the pork.

Genius Tip Creamer potatoes are a variety of potatoes that are harvested before they are mature, keeping them small and tender. They are usually called white or red creamers and are the perfect size for cooking in stew.

Clever, No-Fuss Pizza Crusts

No time for homemade pizza crust or too intimidated to make one? It's time to think beyond traditional crusts and get to pizza faster. Try one of these terrific alternatives!

FOLLOW THE DIRECTIONS BELOW FOR SPECIFIC CRUSTS USING THESE GUIDELINES:

- Heat oven as directed.
- Spray cookie sheet with cooking spray.
- Prebake untopped pizza crust (if necessary) as directed.
- Top with desired toppings.
- Bake as directed until cheese is melted.

PIZZA CRUST	OVEN TEMPERATURE	HOW TO BAKE TOPPED PIZZAS
Bagels (thin), split English muffins, split Naan Pancakes Pita breads Waffles	450°F	Bake: 7 to 12 minutes.
Lavash flatbread Tortillas	425°F	Bake: 8 minutes.
Bread French bread pieces 　(cut lengthwise in 　　half) Garlic bread pieces	425°F	Prebake: 3 to 5 minutes just until lightly toasted. Bake: 10 to 12 minutes.
Frozen bread dough 　(1 lb honey wheat 　　or white, thawed) Purchased pizza dough 　(from pizza restaurant 　　or specialty market)	450°F	Prebake: Pat dough into 12-inch circle on cookie sheet. Prick dough generously with fork. Bake 8 minutes (if dough puffs during baking, flatten with spoon). Bake: 7 to 9 minutes until crust is golden brown.
Purchased prepared 　crust Refrigerated crust		Bake: as directed on package.

German Kielbasa and Cabbage

Prep Time: 40 Minutes • **Start to Finish: 40 Minutes** • **6 servings (1½ cups each)**

4 slices bacon, cut into
½-inch pieces

3 medium red potatoes,
unpeeled, cut into ¾-inch
cubes (3 cups)

1 large onion, coarsely
chopped (1 cup)

1 package (12 oz) kielbasa,
cut in half lengthwise
then crosswise into
1-inch slices

½ cup chicken broth (from
32-oz carton)

¼ cup cider vinegar

5 teaspoons Dijon mustard

1 teaspoon caraway seed

½ large cabbage, coarsely
chopped into 1-inch
pieces (5 cups)

1 cup shredded smoked
Cheddar cheese
or Cheddar cheese (4 oz)

1 tablespoon chopped
fresh parsley

1 In 5- to 6-quart Dutch oven, cook bacon over medium-high heat until crisp. Using slotted spoon, place bacon on paper towel–lined plate; set aside.

2 Add potatoes, onion and kielbasa to drippings in Dutch oven. Cook uncovered 5 minutes, stirring frequently, or until onion is tender.

3 Add chicken broth, vinegar, mustard and caraway seed. Heat to boiling; reduce heat to low. Cover; simmer 8 minutes, stirring occasionally.

4 Add cabbage; stir well. Cover; cook an additional 10 to 12 minutes, stirring occasionally, until potatoes are fork-tender and cabbage is crisp-tender. Remove from heat. Stir in bacon; sprinkle with cheese. Let stand 1 to 2 minutes or until cheese is melted. Sprinkle with parsley.

1 Serving: Calories 410; Total Fat 24g (Saturated Fat 10g, Trans Fat 0.5g); Cholesterol 60mg; Sodium 950mg; Total Carbohydrate 30g (Dietary Fiber 5g); Protein 16g **Exchanges:** ½ Starch, 1½ Other Carbohydrate, ½ Vegetable, 2 High-Fat Meat, 1½ Fat **Carbohydrate Choices:** 2

Customize It This is a great recipe to make your own. Check out your grocery store for a fun-flavored cooked or smoked sausage to use in place of the kielbasa. Or change it up with a spicy brown mustard or sweet mustard!

Sausage Meatballs with Creamy Tomato Penne

Prep Time: 55 Minutes • Start to Finish: 55 Minutes • 6 servings

1 lb bulk mild Italian sausage

½ cup Italian-style panko crispy bread crumbs

½ cup finely chopped onion

1 egg

1 tablespoon olive oil

3 cups chicken broth (from 32-oz carton)

1 jar (25.5 oz) tomato basil pasta sauce

¾ cup whipping cream

12 oz uncooked penne pasta (3¾ cups)

Shredded Parmesan cheese, if desired

Shredded fresh basil leaves, if desired

1 In large bowl, mix sausage, bread crumbs, onion and egg until well combined. Shape mixture into 12 (2-inch) meatballs.

2 In 5-quart Dutch oven, heat oil over medium heat. Add meatballs; cook 9 to 11 minutes, gently turning occasionally, just until browned on all sides.

3 Stir in broth, pasta sauce and whipping cream; heat to boiling. Stir in pasta; return to boiling. Reduce heat; simmer uncovered 18 to 22 minutes, stirring occasionally, until meatballs are thoroughly cooked and no longer pink in center, pasta is tender and sauce is thickened. Sprinkle with Parmesan cheese and basil.

1 Serving: Calories 670; Total Fat 34g (Saturated Fat 12g, Trans Fat 0g); Cholesterol 95mg; Sodium 1560mg; Total Carbohydrate 68g (Dietary Fiber 5g); Protein 24g **Exchanges:** 2½ Starch, 1½ Other Carbohydrate, 1 Vegetable, 2 High-Fat Meat, 3½ Fat **Carbohydrate Choices:** 4½

Genius Tip To easily turn meatballs, use a spatula and a spoon to gently roll each meatball. Make sure oil is hot before carefully adding meatballs. If meatballs don't release easily from bottom of pan, cook a bit longer before attempting to turn.

Customize It The recipe calls for mild sausage, but if you like spicy food, use hot or spicy sausage instead.

Mediterranean Sausage and Quinoa

Prep Time: 25 Minutes • **Start to Finish: 50 Minutes** • **5 servings (1⅓ cups each)**

2 tablespoons olive oil

1 package (12 oz) fully-cooked chicken Italian sausages, cut into ½-inch slices

1 medium onion, chopped (1 cup)

1 medium yellow bell pepper, coarsely chopped (1 cup)

8 oz uncooked quinoa (1⅓ cups), rinsed, well drained

2⅔ cups reduced-sodium chicken broth (from 32-oz carton)

1 can (15 oz) chick peas (garbanzo beans), drained, rinsed

1½ teaspoons dried oregano leaves

½ teaspoon salt

¼ teaspoon crushed red pepper, if desired

1 cup crumbled feta cheese (4 oz)

1 cup grape tomatoes, halved

½ cup diced seedless cucumber

¼ cup pitted Kalamata olives, halved

Chopped fresh basil leaves, if desired

1 In 5- to 6-quart Dutch oven, heat oil over medium heat. Add sausage, onion and bell pepper. Cook 6 to 7 minutes, stirring occasionally, until vegetables are tender. With slotted spoon, transfer mixture to medium bowl; cover.

2 Add quinoa to Dutch oven; cook 1 to 2 minutes, stirring occasionally, until hot. Slowly stir in broth. Add chick peas, oregano, salt and crushed red pepper. Heat to boiling; reduce heat to low. Cover; simmer 20 to 25 minutes, stirring occasionally, or until liquid is absorbed and quinoa is tender. Stir in sausage and vegetable mixture; cook until thoroughly heated, stirring occasionally.

3 Remove from heat; stir in ½ cup of the cheese. Top with tomatoes, cucumber, olives and remaining cheese. Garnish with basil, if desired.

1 Serving: Calories 520; Total Fat 23g (Saturated Fat 7g, Trans Fat 0g); Cholesterol 80mg; Sodium 1360mg; Total Carbohydrate 51g (Dietary Fiber 8g); Protein 28g **Exchanges:** 3 Starch, 1 Vegetable, 1 Very Lean Meat, ½ Medium-Fat Meat, 1 High-Fat Meat, 2 Fat **Carbohydrate Choices:** 3½

Genius Tip Use mixture as a filling for delicious pita sandwiches.

Genius Tip Rinsing with cold water removes the natural coating from quinoa, which can make it taste bitter.

Easy Sausage Lasagna

1 container (15 oz) whole-milk ricotta cheese

2 cups shredded mozzarella cheese (8 oz)

1 jar (26 oz) tomato basil pasta sauce

2 tablespoons butter

1 lb bulk mild Italian sausage

1 cup diced red onion

1 teaspoon salt

½ teaspoon pepper

4 oz no-boil lasagna noodles (from 8-oz package), broken in 3 pieces

½ cup shredded Parmesan cheese

¼ cup thinly sliced fresh basil leaves

1 Heat oven to 425°F. In medium bowl, mix ricotta and mozzarella cheeses; set aside. Place pasta sauce in large bowl; set aside.

2 In 5-quart ovenproof Dutch oven, melt butter over medium-high heat. Add sausage, onion, salt and pepper; cook 6 to 8 minutes, stirring frequently, until sausage is thoroughly cooked and onion is tender; drain. Stir sausage mixture into sauce in bowl.

3 Spread 2 cups sauce mixture in bottom of same Dutch oven. Top with one-third of the lasagna noodles. Top with half of the ricotta mixture. Pour 1 cup of the reserved sauce mixture over ricotta mixture. Top with another one-third of the lasagna noodles. Top with remaining ricotta mixture. Top with remaining lasagna noodles, and then top with remaining sauce mixture. Sprinkle with Parmesan cheese.

4 Cover; bake 15 minutes. Remove cover; bake 10 to 15 minutes longer or until pasta is tender and mixture is browned on edges. Sprinkle with basil.

1 Serving: Calories 480; Total Fat 29g (Saturated Fat 15g, Trans Fat 0.5g); Cholesterol 80mg; Sodium 1350mg; Total Carbohydrate 27g (Dietary Fiber 2g); Protein 27g **Exchanges:** 1 Starch, ½ Other Carbohydrate, 1 Vegetable, ½ Lean Meat, 1½ Medium-Fat Meat, 1 High-Fat Meat, 2½ Fat **Carbohydrate Choices:** 2

Genius Tip Tuck in any little broken pieces of lasagna noodles with the rest of the broken noodles.

Skinny Italian Sausage Soup

Prep Time: 30 Minutes • **Start to Finish: 55 Minutes** • **10 servings (about 1¼ cups each)**

2 slices bacon

½ lb lean Italian turkey sausage, casings removed

2 large russet potatoes, cut into ½-inch cubes (about 4 cups)

1 large onion, chopped (1 cup)

2 cloves garlic, finely chopped

1 teaspoon Italian seasoning

½ teaspoon salt

¼ teaspoon pepper

¼ teaspoon crushed red pepper flakes

4 cups water

3½ cups reduced-sodium chicken broth (from 32-oz carton)

4 cups chopped fresh kale or Swiss chard leaves

1 can (15 or 19 oz) cannellini beans, drained, rinsed

1 cup fat-free half-and-half or regular half-and-half

1 In 5-quart Dutch oven, cook bacon until crisp; drain on paper towel. Crumble bacon; set aside. Remove and discard drippings from Dutch oven.

2 In same Dutch oven, cook sausage over medium-high heat 6 to 8 minutes, stirring frequently, until no longer pink. Drain well; set aside.

3 Add potatoes, onion, garlic, Italian seasoning, salt, pepper, pepper flakes, water and broth to Dutch oven. Heat to boiling. Reduce heat to low; cook uncovered about 10 minutes, stirring occasionally.

4 Stir in bacon, sausage, kale and beans. Cook 10 to 15 minutes, stirring occasionally, until potatoes and kale are tender. Stir in half-and-half; cook just until heated.

1 Serving: Calories 190; Total Fat 3.5g (Saturated Fat 1g, Trans Fat 0g); Cholesterol 20mg; Sodium 530mg; Total Carbohydrate 29g (Dietary Fiber 4g); Protein 12g **Exchanges:** 2 Starch, 1 Very Lean Meat **Carbohydrate Choices:** 2

Genius Tip If you are counting calories, fat-free half-and-half is a great substitute for the classic product. Look for it near the other dairy products at the grocery store.

Italian Sausage and Tortellini Soup

Prep Time: 20 Minutes • Start to Finish: 45 Minutes • 6 servings (about 2 cups each)

1 lb bulk mild Italian sausage

1 medium onion, chopped

2 medium carrots, chopped

3 cloves garlic, finely chopped

2 cartons (32 oz each) chicken broth

1 package (9 oz) refrigerated cheese-filled tortellini

1 bag (5 oz) baby spinach leaves

1 In 5-quart Dutch oven, cook sausage, onion, carrots and garlic over medium heat 8 to 10 minutes, stirring occasionally, until sausage is thoroughly cooked; drain.

2 Stir in broth; heat to boiling over medium-high heat. Add tortellini. Reduce heat to low; cook 8 to 12 minutes or until tortellini are tender. Stir in spinach; cook 1 to 2 minutes or just until spinach is wilted.

1 Serving: Calories 300; Total Fat 18g (Saturated Fat 7g, Trans Fat 0g); Cholesterol 70mg; Sodium 1560mg; Total Carbohydrate 17g (Dietary Fiber 2g); Protein 16g **Exchanges:** 1 Starch, 1 Vegetable, 1½ High-Fat Meat, 1 Fat **Carbohydrate Choices:** 1

Customize It Shredded Parmesan or Asiago cheese makes a nice garnish for this soup.

Cajun Shrimp and Grits

½ lb cooked andouille sausage, cut lengthwise into fourths, then sliced crosswise into ½-inch pieces

1 cup thinly sliced sweet onion

¾ cup chopped red bell pepper (1 small)

¾ cup chopped green bell pepper (1 small)

12 oz uncooked deveined peeled medium shrimp, thawed if frozen, tail shells removed

1½ teaspoons Cajun seasoning

1 can (15 oz) fire-roasted diced tomatoes, undrained

2 cups water

2 tablespoons butter

½ cup uncooked quick-cooking corn grits

¼ teaspoon salt

½ cup shredded smoked Gouda cheese (2 oz)

1 tablespoon chopped fresh Italian (flat-leaf) parsley

1 In 4-quart saucepan, cook sausage, onion and bell peppers over medium-high heat 5 to 6 minutes, stirring occasionally, until vegetables are crisp-tender. Add shrimp; cook 2 to 3 minutes, stirring frequently, just until shrimp turn pink.

2 Stir in seasoning and tomatoes. Cook, uncovered, 2 to 3 minutes or until tomatoes are thoroughly heated. Spoon mixture into medium bowl; cover with foil.

3 In same 4-quart saucepan, place water and butter. Heat to boiling. Stir in grits and salt; reduce heat to low. Cover; cook 5 to 7 minutes, stirring occasionally, until grits are thickened. Remove from heat. Add cheese; stir until melted.

4 To serve, place ½ cup grits in each serving bowl. Place 1½ cups shrimp mixture next to grits. Sprinkle with parsley.

I Serving: Calories 470; Total Fat 26g (Saturated Fat 11g, Trans Fat 0g); Cholesterol 200mg; Sodium 1430mg; Total Carbohydrate 27g (Dietary Fiber 3g); Protein 32g **Exchanges:** 1 Starch, ½ Other Carbohydrate, 1 Vegetable, 3 Very Lean Meat, 1 High-Fat Meat, 3 Fat **Carbohydrate Choices:** 2

Genius Tip Although any onion can be used for the recipe, sweet onions will add a little sweeter flavor because they lack the pungency typically associated with white or yellow onions. Any of the different varieties—Walla Walla, Maui or Bermuda—can be used interchangeably. Since each variety has a different season, what is available to purchase will change.

Genius Tip Frozen shrimp can be thawed overnight in a covered bowl in the refrigerator. Rinse, drain and pat dry before using in a recipe. For faster thawing, place shrimp in a colander. Place a large bowl in the kitchen sink and fill with cold water. Place colander in the bowl, completely submerging the shrimp. Lift colander from bowl to drain and repeat until shrimp are thawed. Pat dry before using.

Honey-Sesame Shrimp Noodle Bowls

Prep Time: 35 Minutes • Start to Finish: 40 Minutes • 4 servings (1⅓ cups each)

1 package (7 oz) spaghetti, broken in half

¼ cup soy sauce

¼ cup honey

1 tablespoon cornstarch

2 teaspoons chili garlic sauce

2 teaspoons sesame seed

1 teaspoon grated fresh gingerroot

1½ cups ready-to-eat baby-cut carrots, cut in half lengthwise

2 tablespoons water

1 tablespoon sesame oil

1 lb uncooked deveined peeled medium shrimp, thawed if frozen, tail shells removed

1 package (8 oz) fresh sugar snap peas (2½ cups)

2 medium green onions, sliced (2 tablespoons)

Sesame seed, if desired

1 In 4-quart saucepan, cook spaghetti as directed on package. Drain in colander; set aside.

2 Meanwhile, in small bowl, combine soy sauce, honey, cornstarch, chili garlic sauce, 2 teaspoons sesame seed and the gingerroot.

3 In same 4-quart saucepan, combine carrots and water. Cover; cook over medium heat 4 minutes. Add sesame oil; heat 30 seconds. Add shrimp and sugar snap peas; cook uncovered 6 to 7 minutes, stirring frequently, or until shrimp turn pink. Stir in soy mixture; cook, stirring constantly, until mixture is thickened. Cook and stir 2 minutes.

4 Add spaghetti; toss to heat through. Serve in bowls; sprinkle with green onions and sesame seed.

1 Serving: Calories 180; Total Fat 6g (Saturated Fat 1g, Trans Fat 0g); Cholesterol 155mg; Sodium 1210mg; Total Carbohydrate 74g (Dietary Fiber 6g); Protein 32g **Exchanges:** 3 Starch, 1½ Other Carbohydrate, 1 Vegetable, 3 Very Lean Meat, ½ Fat **Carbohydrate Choices:** 5

Genius Tip Look for gingerroot in the produce department of your store. The root (or piece of root) should be firm and moist. Break or cut a piece off, peel the skin with a vegetable peeler and then use a hand-held grater to grate the amount you need. Store any remaining gingerroot, covered, in the refrigerator or grate the rest and freeze in a small covered container.

Customize It Chili garlic sauce is a fiery condiment made with red chiles, garlic, salt, sugar and vinegar. For extra zing, add an extra teaspoon or two to the recipe or drizzle a little bit extra over the top of the bowls just before serving.

30-Minute Beer Cheese Soup

Prep Time: 30 Minutes • Start to Finish: 30 Minutes • 5 servings (1½ cups each)

½ cup butter

¾ cup finely chopped carrots

½ cup finely chopped celery

¼ cup finely chopped onion

1 cup quick-mixing or all-purpose flour

½ teaspoon paprika

⅛ teaspoon black pepper

⅛ teaspoon ground red pepper (cayenne)

3 cups chicken broth (from 32-oz carton)

1 cup whipping cream

4 cups shredded sharp Cheddar cheese (16 oz)

1 can (12 oz) beer

Popped popcorn, if desired

1 In 4-quart Dutch oven, melt butter over medium heat. Add carrots, celery and onion; cook about 10 minutes, stirring occasionally, until celery and onions are tender.

2 Stir in flour, paprika, black pepper and ground red pepper. Add broth; heat to boiling over medium heat. Boil and stir 1 minute.

3 Reduce heat; stir in whipping cream and cheese. Heat until cheese is melted, stirring occasionally. Stir in beer. Serve with popcorn.

1 Serving: Calories 790; Total Fat 64g (Saturated Fat 40g, Trans Fat 2g); Cholesterol 195mg; Sodium 1240mg; Total Carbohydrate 26g (Dietary Fiber 1g); Protein 28g **Exchanges:** 1½ Starch, 3½ High-Fat Meat, 7 Fat **Carbohydrate Choices:** 2

Customize It Popped popcorn is the classic garnish for beer cheese soup. But if you have crisp croutons, they are good sprinkled on top, too.

West African Lentil and Vegetable Stew

Prep Time: 20 Minutes • Start to Finish: 40 Minutes • 6 servings (1⅓ cups each)

2 tablespoons vegetable oil

1 medium dark-orange sweet potato, peeled, cut into ½-inch cubes (2 cups)

1 large onion, chopped (1 cup)

2 cloves garlic, finely chopped

3 cups water

1½ cups mild chunky-style salsa (from 16-oz jar)

1½ cups frozen roasted whole kernel corn

1 cup dried lentils, sorted, rinsed

2 medium zucchini, cut in half lengthwise, then cut crosswise into ½-inch slices (2 cups)

1 tablespoon grated gingerroot

2 teaspoons chili powder

1 teaspoon salt

⅛ teaspoon ground red pepper (cayenne)

¼ cup peanut butter

6 tablespoons roasted salted hulled pumpkin seeds (pepitas)

6 sprigs fresh parsley, if desired

1 In 5-quart Dutch oven or 4-quart saucepan, heat oil over medium heat. Add sweet potato, onion and garlic; cook 3 to 4 minutes, stirring occasionally, or until onion is tender.

2 Add water, salsa, corn, lentils, zucchini, gingerroot, chili powder, salt and red pepper; mix well. Heat to boiling; reduce heat. Cover and simmer about 30 minutes, stirring occasionally, until lentils and sweet potatoes are tender. Stir in peanut butter.

3 Divide stew evenly among 6 bowls. Top each serving with 1 tablespoon pumpkin seeds and parsley sprig.

1 Serving: Calories 370; Total Fat 15g (Saturated Fat 2.5g, Trans Fat 0g); Cholesterol 0mg; Sodium 890mg; Total Carbohydrate 43g (Dietary Fiber 10g); Protein 16g **Exchanges:** 1½ Starch, 1 Other Carbohydrate, 1 Vegetable, 1½ Very Lean Meat, 2½ Fat **Carbohydrate Choices:** 3

Customize It Topping each serving with a dollop of plain yogurt or sour cream complements this flavor-packed dish.

Genius Tip Lentils absorb liquid as they cook, so if the stew becomes too thick, just stir in a little additional water. Or if you have leftovers and the stew has thickened, just add a little water before reheating.

Sheet Pan

Parmesan Chicken Fingers and Roasted Veggies

Prep Time: 15 Minutes • Start to Finish: 40 Minutes • 4 servings

¾ lb baby red creamer potatoes, quartered

3 tablespoons olive oil

¾ teaspoon salt

¼ teaspoon seasoned pepper

2 cups fresh broccoli florets

1 clove garlic, finely chopped

⅓ cup Italian-style panko crispy bread crumbs

2 tablespoons all-purpose flour

2 tablespoons grated Parmesan cheese

1 egg

1 package (14 oz) boneless skinless chicken breast tenders

Chopped fresh Italian (flat-leaf) parsley, if desired

1 Heat oven to 450°F. Line half of 18×13-inch half-sheet pan with foil. In medium bowl, combine potatoes, 1 tablespoon of the oil, ¼ teaspoon of the salt and the seasoned pepper until well coated. Spoon potato mixture on unlined side of sheet pan.

2 Roast uncovered 8 minutes.

3 Meanwhile, in same bowl, combine broccoli, garlic, 1 tablespoon of the oil and ¼ teaspoon salt until coated. In large resealable food-storage plastic bag, mix bread crumbs, flour, Parmesan cheese and remaining ¼ teaspoon salt. In small bowl, beat egg.

4 Dip chicken tenders in egg; place in bag with bread crumb mixture. Seal bag; shake to coat evenly. Place chicken tenders on foil-lined side of pan; drizzle with remaining 1 tablespoon oil. Stir broccoli mixture into potatoes on pan.

5 Roast uncovered 10 to 12 minutes or until chicken is no longer pink and potatoes are fork-tender. Sprinkle with parsley.

1 Serving: Calories 380; Total Fat 16g (Saturated Fat 3.5g, Trans Fat 0g); Cholesterol 110mg; Sodium 750mg; Total Carbohydrate 28g (Dietary Fiber 3g); Protein 29g **Exchanges:** 1 Starch, ½ Other Carbohydrate, 1 Vegetable, 3 Very Lean Meat, ½ Medium-Fat Meat, 2½ Fat **Carbohydrate Choices:** 2

Genius Tip Using a bag to coat the chicken is less messy and makes cleanup a breeze.

Genius Tip Make sure broccoli florets are of equal size to ensure even cooking.

Tuscan Chicken Breasts and Vegetables

Prep Time: 20 Minutes • Start to Finish: 1 Hour • 4 servings

¼ cup olive oil

2 tablespoons balsamic vinegar

1 tablespoon finely chopped garlic

1 tablespoon Italian seasoning

1 teaspoon salt

4 boneless skinless chicken breasts (1¾ lb)

4 plum (Roma) tomatoes, halved lengthwise

2 medium zucchini, cut into 2-inch pieces

1 medium red bell pepper, cut into strips

1 cup thinly sliced red onion

1 can (19 oz) cannellini beans, drained, rinsed

½ cup shredded Parmesan cheese

¼ cup thinly sliced fresh basil leaves

1 Heat oven to 425°F. Spray 18×13-inch half-sheet pan with cooking spray. In large bowl, mix oil, vinegar, garlic, Italian seasoning and salt. Pour 2 tablespoons of the mixture into medium bowl. Add chicken; toss to coat. Cover and refrigerate. Add tomatoes, zucchini, bell pepper, onion and beans to remaining mixture in large bowl; toss. Pour vegetable mixture on sheet pan.

2 Roast uncovered 15 minutes.

3 Add chicken to pan with vegetables. Roast uncovered 20 to 25 minutes or until juice of chicken is clear when center of thickest part is cut (at least 165°F) and vegetables are tender.

4 Top with Parmesan cheese and basil leaves.

1 Serving: Calories 610; Total Fat 25g (Saturated Fat 6g, Trans Fat 0g); Cholesterol 135mg; Sodium 1190mg; Total Carbohydrate 36g (Dietary Fiber 9g); Protein 61g **Exchanges:** 1½ Starch, 2 Vegetable, 7 Very Lean Meat, ½ Lean Meat, 4 Fat **Carbohydrate Choices:** 2½

Customize It Mix it up! Try different cheeses and herbs, such as Asiago and 1 tablespoon chopped marjoram.

Genius Tip If you want to remove stems from tomatoes, using a paring knife, make 3 cuts to make a triangle around the stem, then gently pop out the stem with the knife.

Lemon Chicken and Potatoes

Prep Time: 10 Minutes • Start to Finish: 55 Minutes • 4 servings

CHICKEN AND POTATOES

2 tablespoons olive oil

2 teaspoons Greek seasoning

1 lb small new potatoes, quartered

2 tablespoons green goddess dressing

4 boneless skinless chicken breasts (1½ lb)

1 tablespoon honey

4 cups fresh baby spinach

TOPPINGS, IF DESIRED

Sliced lemon

Sliced red onion

Crumbled feta cheese

Chopped fresh oregano leaves

1 Heat oven to 425°F. Spray 18×13-inch half-sheet pan with cooking spray. In large bowl, mix oil and 1 teaspoon of the Greek seasoning. Add potatoes; toss to coat. Place potatoes skin sides down in single layer on sheet pan.

2 Roast uncovered 16 to 18 minutes or until potatoes are just tender when pierced with knife. Remove pan from oven; stir.

3 In same large bowl, mix dressing and remaining 1 teaspoon Greek seasoning. Add chicken to mixture; toss to coat. Arrange in single layer in pan next to potatoes.

4 Roast 20 to 25 minutes longer or until juice of chicken is clear when center of thickest part is cut (at least 165°F) and potatoes are browned and very tender.

5 Drizzle chicken and potatoes with honey. Add spinach to pan. Roast 1 to 2 minutes longer or until spinach wilts slightly. Serve with toppings.

1 Serving: Calories 410; Total Fat 16g (Saturated Fat 3g, Trans Fat 0g); Cholesterol 105mg; Sodium 690mg; Total Carbohydrate 25g (Dietary Fiber 2g); Protein 41g **Exchanges:** 1 Starch, ½ Other Carbohydrate, 1 Vegetable, 5 Very Lean Meat, 2½ Fat **Carbohydrate Choices:** 1½

Genius Tip Chicken breasts vary widely. To ensure all chicken is thoroughly cooked, use an instant-read thermometer to test the temperature of the largest breast in the thickest part. It should read at least 165°F.

Genius Tip Starting the potatoes skin side down keeps them from sticking to the cold sheet pan at the beginning of cooking. To get some browning on the flesh sides of the potatoes, turn each potato piece flesh side down after stirring, just before adding chicken to pan. At this point, the pan is hot and the flesh sides of the potatoes won't stick.

Teriyaki Chicken and Pineapple Stir-Fry

Prep Time: 15 Minutes • Start to Finish: 35 Minutes • 4 servings

¼ cup teriyaki sauce

1 tablespoon honey

1 tablespoon Sriracha sauce

3 boneless skinless chicken breasts, cut into 1-inch chunks

1½ cups 1-inch cubes fresh pineapple

2 medium carrots, cut diagonally into ½-inch slices

1 medium red bell pepper, thinly sliced

1 teaspoon sesame seed

3 green onions, thinly sliced

1 Heat oven to 450°F. Spray 18×13-inch half-sheet pan with cooking spray. In large bowl, beat teriyaki sauce, honey and Sriracha sauce with whisk. Add chicken, pineapple, carrots and bell pepper; gently toss to coat. Arrange in single layer on sheet pan.

2 Roast 14 to 16 minutes or until chicken is no longer pink in center (at least 165°F). Serve immediately, garnished with sesame seed and green onions.

1 Serving: Calories 250; Total Fat 5g (Saturated Fat 1g, Trans Fat 0g); Cholesterol 75mg; Sodium 860mg; Total Carbohydrate 22g (Dietary Fiber 3g); Protein 30g **Exchanges:** ½ Fruit, ½ Other Carbohydrate, 1 Vegetable, 4 Very Lean Meat, ½ Fat **Carbohydrate Choices:** 1½

Find It You can trim a whole pineapple and cut into cubes, or you can buy the precut fresh pineapple sold in the produce section of most grocery stores.

Make It a Meal Steamed white or brown rice would make a nice accompaniment to this dish.

Chicken Fried Rice

Prep Time: 20 Minutes • Start to Finish: 1 Hour • 6 servings

1 package (20 oz) boneless skinless chicken thighs, cut into 1-inch pieces

3 tablespoons thick teriyaki sauce

2½ teaspoons chili garlic sauce

1 tablespoon chopped garlic

2 cups matchstick carrots (from 10-oz package)

6 green onions, thinly sliced, whites and greens separated (about ½ cup)

2 packages (10 oz each) frozen cooked long-grain white rice, heated as directed on packages (about 4 cups cooked rice)

½ cup frozen peas, thawed

¼ cup soy sauce

1 tablespoon vegetable oil

6 eggs

2 teaspoons toasted sesame seed

Sriracha sauce, if desired

1 Heat oven to 450°F. Generously spray 18×13-inch half-sheet pan with cooking spray. In medium bowl, mix chicken, teriyaki sauce, 1½ teaspoons of the chili garlic sauce and the garlic. Place chicken mixture on sheet pan, spreading evenly.

2 Roast uncovered 7 to 9 minutes, stirring halfway through bake time, until chicken is no longer pink in center. Remove mixture from pan to small bowl; cover and keep warm.

3 Spread carrots and whites of green onions evenly on sheet pan. Roast uncovered 6 to 8 minutes or until vegetables are just tender.

4 In medium bowl, mix rice, peas, soy sauce, oil and remaining 1 teaspoon chili garlic sauce. Add rice mixture to vegetable mixture in pan; mix well, spreading evenly. Roast 8 to 10 minutes or until rice starts to brown. Stir in chicken. Make 6 indentations in rice mixture. Gently crack 1 egg into each indentation.

5 Roast uncovered 7 to 9 minutes or until egg yolk and whites are firm. Garnish with sesame seed and greens of green onion. Drizzle with Sriracha sauce.

1 Serving: Calories 380; Total Fat 13g (Saturated Fat 3.5g, Trans Fat 0g); Cholesterol 275mg; Sodium 1490mg; Total Carbohydrate 34g (Dietary Fiber 2g); Protein 30g **Exchanges:** 2 Starch, 1 Vegetable, 2 Very Lean Meat, 1 Medium-Fat Meat, 1 Fat **Carbohydrate Choices:** 2

Customize It If you like heat, stir in another teaspoon of chili garlic sauce.

Sweet Chili Shredded Turkey and Roasted Veggie Sliders

Prep Time: 30 Minutes • Start to Finish: I Hour 25 Minutes • 6 servings

I bone-in turkey breast half
(2 to 2½ lb)

3 tablespoons olive oil

1½ teaspoons kosher
(coarse) salt

¼ teaspoon pepper

3 large red, yellow or
orange bell peppers,
cut into ¼-inch rings

I medium onion, cut into
¼-inch rings

3 cloves garlic, sliced

¼ teaspoon crushed red
pepper, if desired

¾ cup chili sauce (from
12-oz bottle)

4 medium green onions,
thinly sliced (¼ cup)

12 slider buns

Additional chili sauce,
if desired

1 Heat oven to 425°F. Line 18×13-inch half-sheet pan with foil. Rub turkey breast with I tablespoon of the oil; sprinkle with I teaspoon of the salt and the pepper. Place turkey breast, skin side up, on sheet pan.

2 Roast uncovered 25 minutes.

3 Meanwhile, in large bowl, combine bell peppers, onion, garlic, crushed red pepper, remaining ½ teaspoon salt and remaining 2 tablespoons oil; toss to coat. Spoon vegetable mixture in single layer with turkey on sheet pan.

4 Roast 25 to 30 minutes or until meat thermometer inserted in thickest part of breast reads 165°F.

5 Cover turkey and vegetables; let rest 15 minutes. Place turkey on large cutting board; remove and discard skin and bones. Shred meat with 2 forks. Place in microwavable bowl; stir in chili sauce and green onions. Cover with plastic wrap.

6 Microwave turkey mixture on High I to 2 minutes, stirring once. Spoon turkey mixture and roasted vegetables evenly on slider buns.

I Serving: Calories 440; Total Fat 13g (Saturated Fat 2.5g, Trans Fat 0g); Cholesterol 80mg; Sodium 1400mg; Total Carbohydrate 44g (Dietary Fiber 4g); Protein 37g **Exchanges:** 2½ Starch, I Vegetable, 4 Very Lean Meat, 2 Fat **Carbohydrate Choices:** 3

Genius Tip To toast the slider buns, place buns, cut sides down, on cookie sheet. Bake in a 350°F oven until heated, about 5 minutes. Buns may be toasted 30 minutes to an hour ahead of time.

Customize It For more heat, add ¼ teaspoon crushed red pepper flakes to the chili sauce.

Asian Barbecued Chicken with Vegetables

Prep Time: 20 Minutes • Start to Finish: 50 Minutes • 4 servings

½ cup hoisin sauce

2 tablespoons unseasoned rice vinegar

1 tablespoon plus 2 teaspoons Sriracha sauce

4 teaspoons toasted sesame oil

1 teaspoon grated gingerroot

1 clove garlic, finely chopped

1 tablespoon honey

1 tablespoon vegetable oil

2 teaspoons sesame seed

¾ teaspoon salt

1½ cups ready-to-eat baby-cut carrots

8 bone-in chicken thighs, skin removed (about 3 lb)

¼ teaspoon pepper

3 cups broccoli florets (about 7 oz)

1 Heat oven to 425°F. Spray 18×13-inch half-sheet pan with cooking spray. In small bowl, mix hoisin sauce, rice vinegar, 1 tablespoon of the Sriracha sauce, 2 teaspoons of the sesame oil, the gingerroot and garlic. Reserve ¼ cup of hoisin mixture in custard cup to brush on chicken just before serving.

2 In another small bowl, beat honey, vegetable oil, remaining 2 teaspoons Sriracha sauce, remaining 2 teaspoons sesame oil, the sesame seed and ¼ teaspoon of the salt with whisk. In medium bowl, mix half of the honey mixture with carrots. Reserve remaining honey mixture.

3 Sprinkle chicken with remaining ½ teaspoon salt and the pepper. Place chicken on 1 side of sheet pan; brush both sides of chicken with hoisin mixture; reserve remaining mixture. Add carrots in single layer to other side of pan. Roast uncovered 10 minutes.

4 Meanwhile, in medium bowl, toss broccoli with remaining honey mixture.

5 Brush top of chicken thighs with remaining hoisin mixture. Add broccoli to carrots on pan.

6 Roast 15 to 20 minutes or until juice of chicken is clear when thickest part is cut to bone (at least 165°F) and vegetables are lightly browned and just tender. Brush reserved ¼ cup hoisin mixture (in custard cup) on chicken just before serving.

1 Serving: Calories 510; Total Fat 21g (Saturated Fat 4.5g, Trans Fat 0g); Cholesterol 225mg; Sodium 1310mg; Total Carbohydrate 28g (Dietary Fiber 4g); Protein 51g **Exchanges:** 1 Starch, ½ Other Carbohydrate, 1 Vegetable, 6½ Very Lean Meat, 3½ Fat **Carbohydrate Choices:** 2

Genius Tip Hoisin sauce is a thick, sweet and salty sauce, commonly used in Chinese cuisine as a glaze for meat, an addition to stir-fries, or as dipping sauce.

Genius Tip For an easy way to peel gingerroot, just scrape the tip of a teaspoon across the skin, and it should peel off easily.

Jerk Chicken with Sweet Potatoes

Prep Time: 15 Minutes • Start to Finish: 55 Minutes • 4 servings

¼ cup olive oil

1 tablespoon finely chopped gingerroot

1 tablespoon ground jerk seasoning

1 teaspoon soy sauce

¾ teaspoon salt

4 boneless skinless chicken breasts (1¾ lb)

3 medium sweet potatoes, peeled, cut into 1-inch pieces (about 4 cups)

¼ cup chopped fresh cilantro

1 lime, cut into wedges

1 Heat oven to 425°F. Spray 18×13-inch half-sheet pan with cooking spray. In large bowl, mix oil, gingerroot, jerk seasoning, soy sauce and salt. Pour 2 tablespoons of the mixture into medium bowl. Add chicken, and toss to coat; cover and refrigerate. Add sweet potatoes to remaining mixture in bowl; toss. Pour potato mixture onto pan.

2 Roast uncovered 15 minutes.

3 Add chicken to sheet pan with potatoes.

4 Roast uncovered 20 to 25 minutes or until chicken is no longer pink in center (at least 165°F) and potatoes are tender. Top with cilantro. Serve with lime wedges.

1 Serving: Calories 420; Total Fat 19g (Saturated Fat 3.5g, Trans Fat 0g); Cholesterol 100mg; Sodium 860mg; Total Carbohydrate 23g (Dietary Fiber 3g); Protein 39g **Exchanges:** 1½ Starch, 5 Very Lean Meat, 3 Fat **Carbohydrate Choices:** 1½

Customize It For a spicier dish, add a tablespoon of finely chopped hot pepper, such as jalapeño or serrano, to the sauce mixture.

Genius Tip If you don't have an 18×13-inch half-sheet pan, consider investing in one. They're large enough to accommodate a full dinner on 1 pan, but small enough to fit in most home ovens.

Deviled Chicken with Roasted Vegetables

Prep Time: 20 Minutes • Start to Finish: I Hour 10 Minutes • 4 servings

⅓ cup Dijon mustard

1 medium shallot, finely chopped

¼ to ½ teaspoon ground red pepper (cayenne)

¾ teaspoon salt

½ teaspoon pepper

4 bone-in chicken breast halves, skin removed

¾ cup plain panko crispy bread crumbs

½ cup shredded Parmesan cheese

3 tablespoons butter, melted

3 medium Yukon Gold potatoes, each cut into 6 chunks

3 medium carrots, peeled and cut into 2-inch pieces

1 medium leek, trimmed, washed thoroughly and cut crosswise into ½-inch slices

3 tablespoons olive oil

1 Heat oven to 425°F. In small bowl, stir mustard, shallot, red pepper, ¼ teaspoon of the salt and ¼ teaspoon of the pepper until combined. Spread tops of chicken breasts generously with mustard mixture.

2 In shallow bowl, mix bread crumbs, Parmesan cheese and melted butter. Coat chicken in crumbs, patting firmly onto tops and sides of chicken breasts. Place on 1 side of ungreased 18×13-inch half-sheet pan.

3 In large bowl, mix potatoes, carrots, leek, oil and remaining ½ teaspoon salt and ¼ teaspoon pepper. Arrange vegetables in single layer on other side of pan.

4 Roast uncovered 30 to 35 minutes, stirring vegetables once, until chicken is browned and juice is clear when thickest part is cut to bone (at least 165°F). With tongs, transfer chicken to serving plate. Roast vegetables 10 to 15 minutes longer or until tender and lightly browned.

1 Serving: Calories 690; Total Fat 30g (Saturated Fat 11g, Trans Fat 0.5g); Cholesterol 135mg; Sodium 1370mg; Total Carbohydrate 55g (Dietary Fiber 6g); Protein 50g **Exchanges:** 3 Starch, 1½ Vegetable, 4½ Very Lean Meat, 1 Lean Meat, 4½ Fat **Carbohydrate Choices:** 3½

Customize It If you like a little extra spice in your deviled chicken, feel free to up the amount of ground red pepper in the mustard mixture to ½ teaspoon.

Genius Tip Leeks are grown in sandy soil, and dirt can often get trapped in between their long leaves. To trim and clean them, remove all the dark green tops of the leaves, leaving only the pale green and white parts. Cut them in half lengthwise, and thoroughly rinse under cold water, opening up the leaves in the process to release any dirt.

Easy Beef Fajitas

Prep Time: 15 Minutes • Start to Finish: 40 Minutes • 4 servings

FAJITAS

- 2 cups sliced onions
- 1 medium red or yellow bell pepper, cut into ¼-inch strips
- 2 tablespoons vegetable oil
- 1 package (1 oz) taco seasoning mix
- 1 lb boneless beef sirloin steak
- 8 flour tortillas for soft tacos & fajitas (6 inch)

TOPPINGS, IF DESIRED

- Sour cream
- Chunky-style salsa
- Chopped fresh cilantro
- Lime wedges

1 Heat oven to 400°F. Spray 18×13-inch half-sheet pan with cooking spray. Place onion and bell pepper on sheet pan. Add 1 tablespoon of the oil and 2 tablespoons of the taco seasoning mix; stir to coat, spreading mixture evenly in pan.

2 Roast uncovered 15 minutes. Stir.

3 Meanwhile, cut steak into ¼-inch strips; place in small bowl. Stir in remaining 1 tablespoon oil and remaining seasoning mix until combined and coated. Place on sheet pan with vegetables.

4 Roast uncovered 7 to 9 minutes or until beef is no longer pink and vegetables are tender.

5 Heat tortillas as directed on package. Using tongs, transfer steak mixture to serving platter. Spoon steak and vegetables onto each tortilla. Serve with toppings.

1 Serving: Calories 390; Total Fat 15g (Saturated Fat 4.5g, Trans Fat 0g); Cholesterol 65mg; Sodium 830mg; Total Carbohydrate 35g (Dietary Fiber 2g); Protein 28g **Exchanges:** 2 Starch, 1 Vegetable, 3 Lean Meat, 1 Fat **Carbohydrate Choices:** 2

Customize It Feel free to use your favorite bell pepper, and add color by choosing a variety like yellow, red and orange.

Genius Tip You may notice some liquid on the sheet pan after baking, which is completely normal. Simply pour off the liquid, if desired.

Stuffed Peppers 4 Ways

Here's a super way to customize your supper! Pick your peppers, using whatever you have on hand, what's on sale at the grocery store or in season at the farmers' market. You can even mix and match pepper colors for an eye-catching presentation. Next, pick the filling you want; bake and enjoy. Everyone gets their own delicious, delightful dinner!

MIX-AND-MATCH:
PICK A PEPPER OR CHILE + PICK A FILLING (BELOW)

4   large (any color) bell peppers
    (about 2 lbs)
    —OR—
5   large (6×3 inches long) poblano
    chiles (1½ lb)

1 Heat oven to 425°F. Line an 18×13-inch half-sheet pan with parchment paper.

BELL PEPPERS: Cut each bell pepper in half lengthwise.

CHILES: Remove 3×5-inch lengthwise strip from each chile to create a boat. Chop remaining chile pieces; set aside.

Remove seeds and membranes from peppers or chiles; place, cut side up, on sheet pan.

2 Prepare desired filling (see individual recipes, page 134–135). Divide mixture evenly among peppers or chiles. Spray foil with cooking spray; cover pan tightly with foil, sprayed side down. Bake as directed.

3 Top with additional ingredients and bake longer, if necessary (see individual recipes, page 134–135). Let stand 5 minutes before serving. Makes 4 servings (2 bell pepper halves each) or 5 servings (1 chile each).

Stuffed Peppers 4 Ways

Choose one of these fillings; prepare as directed and follow the specific directions for each filling recipe:

Loaded Potato

- 4 oz cream cheese, softened
- ⅔ cup sour cream
- ¼ cup milk
- ½ teaspoon salt
- ¼ teaspoon pepper
- 1 package (20 oz) refrigerated shredded hash brown potatoes
- 1⅓ cups shredded Cheddar cheese
- 12 slices bacon, crisply cooked, crumbled (1 cup)
- 6 medium green onions, thinly sliced (⅓ cup)

1 Heat oven to 425°F. Line 18×13-inch half-sheet pan with cooking parchment paper. Cut each bell pepper in half lengthwise or remove 3×5-inch lengthwise strip from each chile to create a boat. Remove seeds and membranes; place peppers, cut side up, on sheet pan.

2 In large bowl, mix cream cheese, sour cream, milk, salt and pepper; beat with electric mixer on low speed 1 minute or until smooth. Stir in potatoes, 1 cup of the Cheddar cheese, the bacon and ¼ cup of the green onions until mixed well.

3 Divide mixture evenly among peppers (peppers will be full). Spray 1 side of foil piece with cooking spray; cover pan with foil, sprayed side down.

4 Bake 45 minutes. Uncover; sprinkle with remaining ⅓ cup Cheddar cheese. Bake 5 minutes longer or until cheese is melted and bell peppers are fork-tender; let stand 5 minutes. Sprinkle with remaining green onions.

1 Serving (using bell peppers): Calories 630; Total Fat 39g (Saturated Fat 20g, Trans Fat 1g); Cholesterol 115mg; Sodium 1160mg; Total Carbohydrate 45g (Dietary Fiber 6g); Protein 23g **Exchanges:** 2 Starch, ½ Other Carbohydrate, 1½ Vegetable, 2 High-Fat Meat, 4½ Fat **Carbohydrate Choices:** 3

Tuna Pot Pie

- 1 can (10½ oz) condensed cream of chicken soup
- ½ teaspoon Italian seasoning
- ¼ teaspoon salt
- ¼ teaspoon pepper
- 1 can (12 oz) albacore tuna in water, drained
- 2 cups frozen mixed vegetables
- 6 medium green onions, thinly sliced (⅓ cup)
- 1¼ cups shredded Cheddar cheese (5 oz)
- 1 sheet frozen puff pastry, thawed (from 17.3-oz package), cut into 8 rectangles
- 2 tablespoons butter, melted
  Chopped fresh Italian (flat-leaf) parsley, if desired

1 Heat oven to 425°F. Line 18×13-inch half-sheet pan with cooking parchment paper. Cut each bell pepper in half lengthwise or remove 3×5-inch lengthwise strip from each chile to create a boat. Remove seeds and membranes; place peppers, cut side up, on sheet pan.

2 In large bowl, combine soup, Italian seasoning, salt and pepper; mix well. Stir in tuna, vegetables, green onions and 1 cup cheese. Divide mixture evenly among peppers (peppers will be full). Spray 1 side of foil with cooking spray; cover pan tightly with foil, sprayed side down.

3 Bake covered 30 minutes. Remove foil. Place 1 puff pastry rectangle on top of each pepper. Brush melted butter over top of pastry.

4 Bake uncovered 15 to 18 minutes or until pastry is golden brown and peppers are fork-tender. Sprinkle remaining ¼ cup cheese on top of pastry. Bake 1 to 2 minutes longer or until cheese is melted. Let stand 5 minutes. Sprinkle with parsley.

1 Serving (using bell peppers): Calories 260; Total Fat 16g (Saturated Fat 6g, Trans Fat 2.5g); Cholesterol 30mg; Sodium 390mg; Total Carbohydrate 16g (Dietary Fiber 2g); Protein 12g **Exchanges:** 1 Other Carbohydrate, ½ Vegetable, 1 Lean Meat, ½ High-Fat Meat, 2 Fat **Carbohydrate Choices:** 1

Buffalo Chicken and Jalapeño

- 4 oz cream cheese, cubed
- ¼ cup buffalo wing sauce
- ¼ teaspoon garlic powder
- 3 cups chopped cooked chicken
- 2 stalks celery, diced (1 cup)
- 12 medium green onions, thinly sliced (¾ cup)
- 1 small jalapeño chile, seeded, chopped
- 1⅓ cups shredded mozzarella cheese
- ¼ cup crumbled blue cheese

1 Heat oven to 425°F. Line 18×13-inch half-sheet pan with cooking parchment paper. Cut each bell pepper in half lengthwise or remove 3×5-inch lengthwise strip from each chile to create a boat. Remove seeds and membranes; place peppers, cut side up, on sheet pan.

2 In large microwavable bowl, mix cream cheese, 3 tablespoons of the buffalo wing sauce and the garlic powder. Microwave on High 45 to 60 seconds until smooth, stirring every 15 seconds. Stir in chicken, celery, green onions, jalapeño chili and 1 cup of the mozzarella cheese.

3 Divide mixture evenly among peppers (peppers will be full). Spray 1 side of foil piece with cooking spray; cover pan with foil, sprayed side down.

4 Bake 45 minutes. Uncover; top with remaining ⅓ cup mozzarella cheese. Bake 5 to 10 minutes longer, until cheese is melted and peppers are crisp-tender when pierced with fork. Let stand 5 minutes before serving.

5 Just before serving, drizzle with remaining 1 tablespoon buffalo sauce. Top peppers with crumbled blue cheese.

1 Serving (using bell peppers): Calories 540; Total Fat 32 (Saturated Fat 15g, Trans Fat 1.5g); Cholesterol 150mg; Sodium 1090mg; Total Carbohydrate 19g (Dietary Fiber 5g); Protein 44g **Exchanges:** ½ Other Carbohydrate, 2 Vegetable, 4 Very Lean Meat, 1½ Medium Fat Meat, 4½ Fat **Carbohydrate Choices:** 1

Southwest Quinoa

- ½ cup uncooked quinoa, rinsed
- ¾ cup water
- ¾ cup medium chunky-style salsa
- 1 teaspoon chili powder
- ½ teaspoon ground cumin
- ½ teaspoon garlic powder
- ½ cup canned black beans, drained, rinsed
- 1 cup frozen southwest-style corn
- 4 medium green onions, thinly sliced (¼ cup)
- 1¼ cups crumbled Cotija or feta cheese
  Chopped fresh cilantro, if desired

1 Heat oven to 425°F. Line 18×13-inch half-sheet pan with cooking parchment paper. Cut each bell pepper in half lengthwise or remove 3×5-inch lengthwise strip from each chile to create a boat. Remove seeds and membranes; place peppers, cut side up, on sheet pan.

2 In large microwavable bowl, combine quinoa and water; cover with plastic wrap. Microwave on High 8 to 9 minutes or until water is absorbed. Fluff quinoa with fork.

3 Stir salsa, chili powder, cumin, garlic powder, reserved chopped chiles, beans, corn, 2 tablespoons of the green onions and 1 cup of the cheese into quinoa.

4 Divide mixture evenly among chiles (chiles will be full). Spray 1 side of foil with cooking spray; cover pan with foil, sprayed side down.

5 Bake 40 to 45 minutes or until chiles are fork-tender. Let stand 5 minutes. Sprinkle with the remaining ¼ cup cheese, the remaining green onions and cilantro.

1 Serving (using poblano chiles): Calories 290; Total Fat 13g (Saturated Fat 6g, Trans Fat 0g); Cholesterol 35mg; Sodium 880mg; Total Carbohydrate 30g (Dietary Fiber 6g); Protein 13g **Exchanges:** 1½ Starch, 1 Vegetable, 1 Medium-Fat Meat, 1½ Fat **Carbohydrate Choices:** 2

Steakhouse-Style Dinner

Prep Time: 20 Minutes • Start to Finish: 55 Minutes • 4 servings

1¾ lb baby Yukon Gold potatoes (about 20), cut in half lengthwise

2 tablespoons olive oil

¾ teaspoon salt

½ teaspoon pepper

¼ cup butter, softened

1 tablespoon finely chopped fresh Italian (flat-leaf) parsley

1 teaspoon finely chopped fresh thyme leaves

1 teaspoon finely chopped garlic

1 lb asparagus, trimmed

4 boneless beef New York strip steaks, ¾ to 1 inch thick (about 2 lb)

4 teaspoons Montreal steak grill seasoning

1 Move one oven rack to center and one 6 inches below broiler. Heat oven to 425°F. Spray 18×13-inch half-sheet pan with cooking spray. In shallow bowl, mix potatoes with 1 tablespoon of the oil, ½ teaspoon of the salt and ¼ teaspoon of the pepper. Place on sheet pan, cut side down.

2 Roast uncovered on center rack 25 to 30 minutes or until potatoes are fork-tender.

3 Meanwhile, in small bowl, mix butter, parsley, thyme, garlic and remaining ¼ teaspoon pepper; set aside. In shallow bowl, mix asparagus, remaining 1 tablespoon oil and remaining ¼ teaspoon salt. Gently toss to combine.

4 Remove sheet pan from oven. Spoon potatoes onto plate; cover to keep warm. Set oven control to broil.

5 Sprinkle each of the steaks with 1 teaspoon grill seasoning; place on same sheet pan. Place pan on top rack; broil steaks 5 minutes. Remove sheet pan from oven, turn steaks over and arrange asparagus around steaks. Place back on top rack; broil 4 to 6 minutes or until steaks are desired doneness (160°F for medium) and asparagus is just tender. Turn oven off.

6 Place steaks on cutting board; let stand 5 minutes. Meanwhile, place potatoes back on sheet pan with asparagus. Place in oven 4 to 5 minutes or until potatoes are warm and asparagus is tender.

7 Spoon dollop of butter mixture on top of each steak. Serve steaks with potatoes and asparagus.

1 Serving: Calories 720; Total Fat 35g (Saturated Fat 14g, Trans Fat 1g); Cholesterol 190mg; Sodium 1930mg; Total Carbohydrate 40g (Dietary Fiber 6g); Protein 61g **Exchanges:** 2 Starch, 1½ Vegetable, 7½ Very Lean Meat, 6 Fat **Carbohydrate Choices:** 2½

Genius Tip Baby potatoes usually are about 1 to 1½ inches in diameter. If your potatoes are larger than that, you may want to cut them into quarters.

Genius Tip Sheet-pan dinners usually have a few moving parts. In this recipe, we roast the potatoes in a hot oven, turn the oven to broil to cook the steaks and asparagus, then turn the oven off and let the potatoes and asparagus keep warm while the steaks rest. The technique isn't difficult, but following the instructions closely will ensure success.

Italian Pork Chop Dinner

Prep Time: 30 Minutes • Start to Finish: 1 Hour 5 Minutes • 4 servings

5 tablespoons butter, melted

1 tablespoon finely chopped garlic

1 tablespoon Italian seasoning

1¼ teaspoons salt

4 bone-in pork loin chops (1½ lb)

2 russet potatoes, unpeeled, cut into 1-inch pieces (1 lb)

½ cup Italian-style panko crispy bread crumbs

¼ cup shredded Parmesan cheese

1 cup cherry tomatoes

½ lb green beans, trimmed

¼ cup thinly sliced fresh basil leaves

1 Heat oven to 425°F. Spray 18×13-inch half-sheet pan with cooking spray. In large bowl, mix 4 tablespoons of the melted butter, the garlic, Italian seasoning and 1 teaspoon of the salt. Pour 2 tablespoons of the mixture into medium bowl. Add pork chops; toss to coat. Cover; refrigerate.

2 Add potatoes to remaining mixture in large bowl; toss. Pour potato mixture onto sheet pan.

3 Roast uncovered 25 to 30 minutes, stirring once, until tender.

4 Meanwhile, in medium bowl, mix remaining 1 tablespoon melted butter, the bread crumbs and Parmesan cheese; set aside.

5 Add pork to sheet pan with potatoes. Top pork with bread crumb mixture; press to adhere. Add tomatoes and green beans to pan; sprinkle vegetables with remaining ¼ teaspoon salt.

6 Roast uncovered 12 to 18 minutes or until pork is no longer pink when cut near bone and potatoes are browned and tender. Sprinkle with basil.

1 Serving: Calories 520; Total Fat 26g (Saturated Fat 14g, Trans Fat 0.5g); Cholesterol 120mg; Sodium 1230mg; Total Carbohydrate 37g (Dietary Fiber 4g); Protein 34g **Exchanges:** 2 Starch, 1½ Vegetable, 3½ Very Lean Meat, 4½ Fat **Carbohydrate Choices:** 2½

Customize It For a little heat, add ¼ teaspoon crushed red pepper flakes to the bread crumb mixture.

Genius Tip For convenience, look for already cleaned bagged green beans.

Bacon-Wrapped Pork Chops and Cauliflower

Prep Time: 20 Minutes • Start to Finish: 45 Minutes • 4 servings

2 packages (10 oz each) fresh cauliflower florets (about 5 cups)

3 tablespoons olive oil

¼ teaspoon salt

¼ teaspoon crushed red pepper

8 strips bacon

4 boneless center-cut pork loin chops, ¾ inch thick (about 1 lb)

1 tablespoon chopped fresh thyme leaves

½ teaspoon finely chopped fresh rosemary leaves

¼ teaspoon black pepper

1 teaspoon finely grated lemon peel

1 Heat oven to 425°F. Spray 18×13-inch half-sheet pan with cooking spray. In large bowl, mix cauliflower, 2 tablespoons of the olive oil, the salt and red pepper. Spread cauliflower mixture evenly on sheet pan.

2 Roast uncovered 20 minutes. Remove from oven; stir well.

3 Meanwhile, place bacon on microwavable plate. Cover; microwave on High 3 to 4 minutes or just until edges begin to brown but are still soft.

4 Rub pork chops with remaining 1 tablespoon olive oil; sprinkle with thyme, rosemary and black pepper. Arrange 2 bacon pieces over top of each pork chop. Place on sheet pan with cauliflower, tucking ends of bacon under each pork chop.

5 Roast uncovered 9 to 11 minutes or until pork is no longer pink when cut near bone. Sprinkle lemon peel over cauliflower.

1 Serving: Calories 370; Total Fat 24g (Saturated Fat 6g, Trans Fat 0g); Cholesterol 80mg; Sodium 500mg; Total Carbohydrate 8g (Dietary Fiber 3g); Protein 31g **Exchanges:** 1½ Vegetable, 3½ Very Lean Meat, ½ High Fat Meat, 3½ Fat **Carbohydrate Choices:** ½

Genius Tip Partially cooking the bacon is necessary to ensure doneness at end of cook time.

Customize It Serve with additional chopped fresh herbs, if desired.

Teriyaki Pork and Vegetables

Prep Time: 15 Minutes • Start to Finish: 45 Minutes • 4 servings

PORK AND RICE

- 1   pork tenderloin (1 lb)
- 1   tablespoon vegetable oil
- ½   teaspoon red pepper flakes
- ¼   cup teriyaki stir-fry sauce and marinade
- 2   cups chicken broth (from 32-oz carton)
- 1   cup uncooked jasmine rice
- ¼   teaspoon salt

VEGETABLES

- ¼   cup Asian sesame dressing (from 8-oz bottle)
- 1   tablespoon soy sauce
- 1   bag (12 oz) California stir-fry vegetables
- ¼   cup thinly sliced green onions

1 Heat oven to 425°F. Spray 15×10-inch rimmed sheet pan with cooking spray. Add pork to sheet pan. Rub with oil and pepper flakes.

2 Roast uncovered 15 minutes. Turn pork. Reserve 2 tablespoons of the teriyaki sauce. Brush pork with remaining 2 tablespoons teriyaki sauce.

3 Meanwhile, in large microwavable bowl, mix broth, rice and salt. Cover with plastic wrap; microwave on High 5 minutes. Stir well. Microwave on Medium (50%) 15 minutes. Let stand covered 5 minutes. Carefully uncover. Stir.

4 In large bowl, mix dressing and soy sauce. Add vegetables; toss to coat. Pour vegetables on sheet pan with pork.

5 Roast uncovered 14 to 16 minutes or until thermometer placed in pork reads 145°F and vegetables are fork-tender. Let stand 5 minutes.

6 Cut pork into slices, and divide among 4 plates. Drizzle pork with remaining 2 tablespoons teriyaki sauce. Divide vegetable mixture among plates; drizzle with pan drippings. Top with green onions. Serve with rice.

1 Serving: Calories 540; Total Fat 15g (Saturated Fat 3g, Trans Fat 0g); Cholesterol 70mg; Sodium 1190mg; Total Carbohydrate 64g (Dietary Fiber 6g); Protein 36g **Exchanges:** 2 Starch, 2 Other Carbohydrate, 1 Vegetable, 4 Lean Meat, ½ Fat **Carbohydrate Choices:** 4

Genius Tip Pork tenderloins vary in size and thickness. If your pork tenderloin finishes cooking before the vegetables are tender, transfer pork to a cutting board, tent with foil and return vegetables to oven for a few more minutes to finish cooking to desired tenderness.

Genius Tip Don't skip the step of trimming the pork tenderloin. That membrane doesn't cook away, and it prevents flavors and seasonings from getting to the meat. To remove silverskin, run a knife underneath the shiny membrane, and slice to remove the silverskin while removing as little meat as possible.

Roasted Pork Tenderloin Dinner

Prep Time: 20 Minutes • Start to Finish: I Hour • 6 servings

2 tablespoons olive oil

4 cloves garlic, finely chopped

I teaspoon dried thyme leaves

I teaspoon salt

½ teaspoon pepper

I pork tenderloin (1½ lb)

I small red onion, cut into ½-inch wedges

I lb Brussels sprouts, halved

I lb small red potatoes, quartered

4 slices thick-sliced bacon, cut into I-inch pieces

1 Heat oven to 425°F. Spray 18×13-inch half-sheet pan with cooking spray. In small bowl, stir oil, garlic, thyme, salt and pepper until well mixed. Place pork in center of pan; rub with I tablespoon of the oil mixture.

2 In large bowl, mix onion, Brussels sprouts, potatoes and remaining I tablespoon oil mixture until well coated. Spoon vegetables around pork. Sprinkle with bacon.

3 Roast uncovered 30 to 35 minutes or until thermometer inserted in pork reads 145°F and vegetables are browned and tender. Let stand 5 minutes.

4 Cut pork into ½-inch-thick slices. Serve with vegetables.

I Serving: Calories 310; Total Fat 12g (Saturated Fat 3g, Trans Fat 0g); Cholesterol 75mg; Sodium 570mg; Total Carbohydrate 21g (Dietary Fiber 4g); Protein 31g **Exchanges:** I Starch, I Vegetable, 3½ Very Lean Meat, 2 Fat **Carbohydrate Choices:** 1½

Customize It
If you like butternut squash, feel free to substitute it for the Brussels sprouts. Already cubed squash can often be found in your supermarket's refrigerated produce section and is a great help to getting dinner on the table fast.

Make It a Meal
Serve this one-pan meal with crusty baguette slices.

Pork with Sweet Potatoes and Apples

Prep Time: 20 Minutes • Start to Finish: 50 Minutes • 4 servings

½ cup butter, melted

1 tablespoon thinly sliced fresh sage leaves

1 teaspoon salt

½ teaspoon pepper

2 medium sweet potatoes, peeled, quartered lengthwise

2 medium Gala apples, cores removed, quartered

1 medium sweet onion, cut into 1-inch pieces

1 pork tenderloin (1 lb)

½ cup real maple syrup

1 tablespoon fresh lemon juice

¼ cup chopped pecans, toasted

1 Heat oven to 425°F. Spray 18×13-inch half-sheet pan with cooking spray. In large bowl, mix melted butter, sage, salt and pepper. Add sweet potatoes, apples and onion; toss to coat. Using tongs or slotted spoon, place on sheet pan in single layer. Add pork to bowl with butter mixture; turn to coat. Add to sheet pan with vegetables.

2 Roast uncovered 23 to 27 minutes or until thermometer inserted in pork reads 145°F and potatoes are fork-tender. Let stand 5 minutes.

3 Meanwhile, in 1½-quart saucepan, heat maple syrup just to boiling over medium heat. Immediately reduce heat to low; cook 7 to 8 minutes or until reduced to ⅓ cup. Remove from heat. Stir in lemon juice. Set aside.

4 Slice pork; divide among 4 plates. Divide potato mixture on plates; drizzle with maple syrup. Top with pecans.

1 Serving: Calories 640; Total Fat 33g (Saturated Fat 17g, Trans Fat 1g); Cholesterol 130mg; Sodium 870mg; Total Carbohydrate 56g (Dietary Fiber 5g); Protein 28g **Exchanges:** 2½ Starch, ½ Fruit, ½ Other Carbohydrate, 3 Lean Meat, 4½ Fat **Carbohydrate Choices:** 4

Genius Tip Try to find half-sheet pans (18×13 inches) for your sheet-pan suppers. They're extremely versatile and allow ample room to fit a whole meal on one pan.

Customize It Feel like experimenting? Instead of pecans, try walnuts or hazelnuts.

Honey-Balsamic Pork Chop Dinner

Prep Time: 30 Minutes • Start to Finish: 1 Hour • 4 servings

3 medium sweet potatoes, peeled, cut into 1-inch pieces (about 4 cups)

2 tablespoons olive oil

1¼ teaspoons salt

½ teaspoon pepper

½ lb fresh broccoli florets (about 4 cups)

4 boneless center-cut pork loin chops (about ¾ inch thick)

3 tablespoons honey

1 tablespoon Dijon mustard

2 teaspoons balsamic vinegar

1 Heat oven to 425°F. Spray 18×13-inch half-sheet pan with cooking spray. In large bowl, mix sweet potatoes, 1 tablespoon of the oil, ½ teaspoon of the salt and ¼ teaspoon of the pepper. Stir to coat. Place on sheet pan.

2 Roast uncovered 25 minutes.

3 In same bowl, mix broccoli, remaining 1 tablespoon oil and ¼ teaspoon of the salt. Remove sheet pan from oven; stir or turn potatoes. Arrange broccoli on pan with potatoes. Roast 5 minutes.

4 Meanwhile, sprinkle pork chops with remaining ½ teaspoon salt and remaining ¼ teaspoon pepper. In small bowl, mix honey, mustard and vinegar. Reserve 2 tablespoons of the honey glaze.

5 Remove sheet pan from oven; add pork chops to pan. Brush pork chops with remaining honey glaze.

6 Roast uncovered 18 to 22 minutes or until pork is no longer pink and meat thermometer inserted in center reads at least 145°F, and vegetables are browned and tender. Let stand 5 minutes.

7 Spoon reserved 2 tablespoons honey glaze on pork chops. Serve pork chops with vegetables.

1 Serving: Calories 470; Total Fat 15g (Saturated Fat 3.5g, Trans Fat 0g); Cholesterol 110mg; Sodium 1000mg; Total Carbohydrate 37g (Dietary Fiber 4g); Protein 44g **Exchanges:** 1½ Starch, ½ Other Carbohydrate, 1 Vegetable, 5½ Very Lean Meat, 2½ Fat **Carbohydrate Choices:** 2½

Genius Tip Make sure to use the red-skinned, orange-fleshed sweet potatoes for this recipe.

Genius Tip We suggest using boneless, ¾-inch pork chops, which is what we based our cook time on; but if your chops are thicker or thinner, you'll need to adjust the cooking time. Using a meat thermometer helps to take the guesswork out of determining when your pork chops are done.

Maple Bratwurst Dinner

Prep Time: 15 Minutes • Start to Finish: 45 Minutes • 4 servings

1 lb small red potatoes, halved

1 cup ready-to-eat baby-cut carrots

2 bell peppers (any color), cut into 1-inch pieces

1 medium onion, cut into wedges

1 tablespoon olive oil

½ teaspoon salt

¼ cup maple-flavored syrup

4 teaspoons spicy brown mustard

1 teaspoon caraway seed

4 smoked bratwurst links, cut crosswise into thirds (12 oz)

1 Heat oven to 425°F. Spray 18×13-inch half-sheet pan with cooking spray. In pan, combine potatoes, carrots, bell peppers and onion. Drizzle with oil; sprinkle with salt. Stir to coat.

2 Roast uncovered 25 minutes.

3 In small bowl, combine maple syrup, mustard and caraway seed; mix well. Add bratwurst to vegetables on pan. Drizzle maple syrup mixture over vegetables and bratwurst. Using spatula or large spoon, carefully mix vegetables and bratwurst to coat.

4 Roast uncovered 10 to 15 minutes or until vegetables are fork-tender.

1 Serving: Calories 480; Total Fat 28g (Saturated Fat 9g, Trans Fat 0.5g); Cholesterol 50mg; Sodium 1190mg; Total Carbohydrate 46g (Dietary Fiber 5g); Protein 13g **Exchanges:** ½ Starch, 2½ Other Carbohydrate, ½ Vegetable, 1½ High-Fat Meat, 3 Fat **Carbohydrate Choices:** 3

Genius Tip Although this recipe is simple, you can get it in the oven in minutes by cutting up the peppers, onions and bratwurst the night before or earlier in the day. Be sure to cover and refrigerate them. The potatoes should be cut just before final preparations because cut sides will brown when exposed to air.

Customize It What's in your refrigerator? Other mustards such as Dijon or honey mustard would be delicious with these flavors.

Bacon and Egg Hash

Prep Time: 35 Minutes • **Start to Finish:** 1 Hour 45 Minutes • **6 servings**

2 medium sweet potatoes, peeled, cut into ¼-inch pieces (about 4 cups)

4 medium red potatoes, cut into ¼-inch pieces (about 3 cups)

1 large red onion, chopped (about 2 cups)

8 slices bacon, chopped

2 tablespoons olive oil

4 cloves garlic, finely chopped

2½ teaspoons finely chopped fresh thyme leaves

1¼ teaspoons salt

¾ teaspoon pepper

6 eggs

2 tablespoons chopped fresh Italian (flat-leaf) parsley

1 Heat oven to 450°F. Spray 18×13-inch half-sheet pan with cooking spray. In large bowl, mix sweet potatoes, red potatoes, onion, bacon, oil, garlic, thyme, 1 teaspoon of the salt and ½ teaspoon of the pepper. Spread in even layer on sheet pan.

2 Bake uncovered 1 hour 5 minutes to 1 hour 15 minutes, stirring every 20 minutes, until bacon is crisp and potatoes are browned.

3 Remove pan from oven; create 6 indentations in potato mixture. Gently crack 1 egg into each indentation; sprinkle eggs with remaining ¼ teaspoon salt and ¼ teaspoon pepper. Bake 6 to 8 minutes or until egg yolk and whites are firm. Sprinkle with parsley.

1 Serving: Calories 340; Total Fat 14g (Saturated Fat 3.5g, Trans Fat 0g); Cholesterol 195mg; Sodium 800mg; Total Carbohydrate 40g (Dietary Fiber 5g); Protein 13g **Exchanges:** 1 Starch, 1 Other Carbohydrate, 1½ Vegetable, 1 Medium-Fat Meat, 1½ Fat **Carbohydrate Choices:** 2½

Customize It Yukon Gold potatoes can be substituted for red potatoes in this recipe.

Genius Tip Make sure to get the red-skinned, orange-fleshed sweet potatoes for this dish.

Baked Caprese Tuna Quesadillas

Prep Time: 20 Minutes • Start to Finish: 50 Minutes • 4 servings

1 package (11 oz) flour tortillas for burritos (8 tortillas, 8 inch)

1 can (12 oz) albacore tuna in water, drained

1 medium plum (Roma) tomato, seeded, chopped (½ cup)

½ cup chopped green bell pepper

¼ cup finely chopped onion

4 tablespoons mayonnaise

6 tablespoons basil pesto

1 ball (8 oz) fresh mozzarella, thinly sliced, cut into small pieces

1 Heat oven to 400°F. Line 18×13-inch half-sheet pan with parchment paper; spray with cooking spray. Place 2 tortillas on pan.

2 In medium bowl, mix tuna, tomato, pepper, onion and 2 tablespoons of the mayonnaise. Spread 1 tablespoon of the pesto on each tortilla on sheet pan. Arrange one-fourth of mozzarella cheese pieces over pesto on each tortilla. Gently spread about ½ cup tuna mixture over each tortilla; top each with another tortilla; spray tops with cooking spray.

3 Bake 10 to 15 minutes or until golden brown. Using pancake turner, carefully transfer quesadillas to serving plates. Cover to keep warm. Repeat with remaining 4 tortillas and tuna mixture. Cut quesadillas into wedges.

4 In small bowl, gently stir remaining mayonnaise and pesto to create swirl design. Serve quesadillas with sauce.

1 Serving: Calories 720; Total Fat 43g (Saturated Fat 15g, Trans Fat 2.5g); Cholesterol 90mg; Sodium 1690mg; Total Carbohydrate 45g (Dietary Fiber 2g); Protein 38g **Exchanges:** 2½ Starch, 1 Vegetable, 2 Lean Meat, 2 Medium-Fat Meat, 5 Fat **Carbohydrate Choices:** 3

Customize It What kind of tortillas do you have on hand? Try spinach, whole-wheat, multigrain or gluten-free tortillas. If you like, substitute 1¼ cups of chopped cooked chicken for the tuna.

Find It We recommend refrigerated basil pesto for the fresh flavor, but you can also find jarred pesto in the grocery aisle (near the pasta). For a different twist, try sun-dried tomato pesto instead of the basil pesto.

Indian-Spiced Salmon Dinner

Prep Time: 20 Minutes • Start to Finish: 1 Hour • 4 servings

⅓ cup vegetable oil

3 cloves garlic, finely chopped

2 teaspoons grated gingerroot

1 tablespoon garam masala

1 teaspoon paprika

1 teaspoon kosher (coarse) salt

¼ teaspoon red pepper flakes

½ head cauliflower, cut into 1-inch florets (2½ cups)

1½ cups ready-to-eat baby-cut carrots, cut in half lengthwise

½ large red onion, cut into 1-inch wedges

1 can (15.5 oz) chick peas (garbanzo beans), drained, rinsed

4 salmon fillets (4 oz each)

2 tablespoons chopped fresh cilantro

1 Heat oven to 425°F. Spray 18×13-inch half-sheet pan with cooking spray. In small bowl, mix oil, garlic, gingerroot, garam masala, paprika, salt and red pepper flakes with whisk; set aside.

2 In large resealable food-storage plastic bag, combine cauliflower, carrots, red onion and chick peas. Add 3 tablespoons of the oil mixture to vegetables in bag. Seal bag; rotate to coat vegetables. Place in single layer on sheet pan.

3 Roast uncovered 20 minutes. Place salmon, skin side down, on sheet pan with vegetables. Brush remaining oil mixture over salmon fillets.

4 Roast 15 to 18 minutes or until salmon flakes easily and vegetables are fork-tender. Sprinkle with cilantro.

1 Serving: Calories 500; Total Fat 29g (Saturated Fat 5g, Trans Fat 0g); Cholesterol 65mg; Sodium 840mg; Total Carbohydrate 27g (Dietary Fiber 8g); Protein 32g **Exchanges:** 1 Other Carbohydrate, 2 Vegetable, 4 Medium-Fat Meat, 2 Fat **Carbohydrate Choices:** 2

Find It Garam masala is actually a flavor-packed blend of up to 12 dry-roasted ground spices. It originated in India and usually contains black pepper, cinnamon, cloves, coriander, cumin, cardamom, dried chiles, fennel, mace and nutmeg. Find it with the other spices in your grocery store.

Genius Tip For super-quick cleanup, line the pan with foil. When dinner is done, simply throw the foil away and give a quick rinse to the pan. That's easy!

Lemon-Garlic Fish and Vegetables

Prep Time: 25 Minutes • Start to Finish: 1 Hour • 4 servings

4 cod fillets (6 oz each)

2 eggs

½ cup all-purpose flour

½ cup shredded Parmesan cheese

2 teaspoons lemon zest

1 teaspoon salt

½ teaspoon pepper

1 lb fresh asparagus

2 medium carrots, cut into 3x½-inch strips (about 1 cup)

1 medium red onion, cut into 1-inch wedges

2 cloves garlic, finely chopped

2 teaspoons chopped fresh thyme leaves or ½ teaspoon dried thyme leaves

3 tablespoons olive oil

Lemon wedges, if desired

1 Heat oven to 400°F. Line 18×13-inch half-sheet pan with foil. Pat cod fillets with paper towel to remove moisture.

2 In shallow dish, beat eggs with fork. In another shallow dish, combine flour, ¼ cup of the Parmesan cheese, the lemon zest, ¼ teaspoon of the salt and ⅛ teaspoon of the pepper until well mixed. Dip each fillet into egg; coat with flour mixture. Place fillets on 1 side of pan.

3 In 2-gallon resealable food-storage plastic bag, combine asparagus, carrots, onion and garlic. Add thyme leaves, the remaining ¾ teaspoon salt, the remaining ⅛ teaspoon pepper and the olive oil. Seal bag; shake until vegetables are well coated. Arrange vegetables in single layer on other side of pan.

4 Bake 30 to 35 minutes or until fillets flake easily with fork and vegetables are crisp-tender. Sprinkle vegetables with the remaining ¼ cup Parmesan cheese. Serve with lemon wedges.

1 Serving: Calories 430; Total Fat 18g (Saturated Fat 5g, Trans Fat 0g); Cholesterol 175mg; Sodium 940mg; Total Carbohydrate 23g (Dietary Fiber 4g); Protein 43g **Exchanges:** ½ Starch, ½ Other Carbohydrate, 1½ Vegetable, 4½ Very Lean Meat, ½ Lean Meat, ½ Medium-Fat Meat, 2½ Fat **Carbohydrate Choices:** 1½

Make It a Meal Round out this delicious fish dinner with your favorite couscous, quinoa or rice pilaf.

Genius Tip Cod is a mild-flavored, firm-flesh fish. Good substitutes for cod are tilapia, walleye or whitefish. Ask the butcher to cut the fillets into serving pieces.

Shrimp Boil Dinner

Prep Time: 15 Minutes • Start to Finish: 50 Minutes • 4 servings

4 tablespoons butter, melted

1½ teaspoons Cajun seasoning

1 lb small new potatoes, quartered

1 package (14 oz) kielbasa sausage, cut into ½-inch slices

1 lb uncooked deveined peeled extra-large shrimp, tails left on

1 cup frozen whole kernel corn (from 10-oz bag)

1 lemon, thinly sliced

1 Heat oven to 425°F. Spray 18×13-inch half-sheet pan with cooking spray. In large bowl, mix 2 tablespoons of the butter and ½ teaspoon of the Cajun seasoning. Add potatoes; toss to coat. Place potatoes, skin side down, in single layer on sheet pan.

2 Roast uncovered 18 to 22 minutes or until very tender when pierced with knife. Remove from oven; stir. Add sausage to potatoes; move to 1 side of pan, making room for shrimp and corn.

3 In same large bowl, mix remaining 2 tablespoons butter and remaining 1 teaspoon Cajun seasoning. Add shrimp, and toss to coat; stir in frozen corn. Arrange in single layer in pan next to potatoes and sausage.

4 Roast uncovered 8 to 10 minutes longer or until shrimp are pink and potatoes are browned and fork-tender. Stir to combine. Top with lemon slices.

1 Serving: Calories 630; Total Fat 41g (Saturated Fat 18g, Trans Fat 1.5g); Cholesterol 265mg; Sodium 2000mg; Total Carbohydrate 34g (Dietary Fiber 4g); Protein 33g **Exchanges:** 2 Starch, 1 Very Lean Meat, 3 High-Fat Meat, 3 Fat **Carbohydrate Choices:** 2

Genius Tip If your new potatoes are large, cut in 6 wedges instead of quartering.

Deconstructed Ratatouille

Prep Time: 20 Minutes • Start to Finish: 1 Hour • 4 servings (1¾ cups each)

1 large eggplant (1 lb),
   peeled, cut into 1-inch
   cubes (about 6 cups)

1 large zucchini, cut
   lengthwise into ½-inch
   slices, then crosswise
   into 1x½-inch strips

1 large summer squash,
   cut into 1x½-inch strips

1 large red or orange
   bell pepper, cut into
   1-inch pieces

2 cups grape tomatoes

2 tablespoons olive oil

1 teaspoon Italian
   seasoning

1 teaspoon garlic salt

½ teaspoon pepper

¼ cup Italian-style panko
   crispy bread crumbs

¼ cup shredded
   Parmesan cheese

1 Heat oven to 400°F. On 18x13-inch half-sheet pan, place eggplant, zucchini, summer squash, bell pepper and tomatoes. Drizzle with oil; sprinkle with Italian seasoning, garlic salt and pepper. Toss until well coated.

2 Roast 25 to 30 minutes, stirring once until vegetables are crisp-tender.

3 In small bowl, mix bread crumbs and Parmesan cheese; sprinkle evenly over eggplant mixture.

4 Roast 5 to 10 minutes longer or until crumbs are golden brown.

1 Serving: Calories 210; Total Fat 10g (Saturated Fat 2.5g, Trans Fat 0g); Cholesterol 0mg; Sodium 470mg; Total Carbohydrate 24g (Dietary Fiber 7g); Protein 7g **Exchanges:** ½ Other Carbohydrate, 3½ Vegetable, 2 Fat **Carbohydrate Choices:** 1½

Customize It Serve this flavorful ratatouille over cooked brown rice and top with crumbled chèvre (goat) or feta cheese.

Customize It For a heartier ratatouille with a bit more protein, just add rinsed and drained garbanzo beans to the eggplant mixture before baking.

Slow Cooker

Buffalo Chicken Chili

Prep Time: 15 Minutes • Start to Finish: 8 Hours 15 Minutes • 6 servings (1½ cups each)

2½ lb boneless skinless chicken thighs, cut into 1-inch pieces

1 large onion, chopped (about 1 cup)

2 medium stalks celery, sliced (about 1 cup)

2 medium carrots, chopped (about 1 cup)

1 can (28 oz) diced tomatoes, undrained

1 can (15 oz) black beans, drained, rinsed

1 cup chicken broth (from 32-oz carton)

2 teaspoons chili powder

½ teaspoon salt

¼ cup buffalo wing sauce (from 12-oz jar)

Crumbled blue cheese, if desired

1 Spray 5- to 6-quart slow cooker with cooking spray. In cooker, mix all ingredients except buffalo wing sauce and cheese.

2 Cover; cook on Low heat setting 8 to 10 hours.

3 Stir in buffalo wing sauce. Serve sprinkled with blue cheese.

1 Serving: Calories 370; Total Fat 10g (Saturated Fat 3g, Trans Fat 0g); Cholesterol 180mg; Sodium 1060mg; Total Carbohydrate 24g (Dietary Fiber 7g); Protein 45g **Exchanges:** 1½ Other Carbohydrate, 1 Vegetable, 3 Very Lean Meat, 3 Lean Meat **Carbohydrate Choices:** 1½

Customize It If you don't have buffalo wing sauce, you can use a mixture of ½ teaspoon red pepper sauce and ¼ teaspoon ground red pepper (cayenne).

Make It a Meal If you choose not to serve this soup sprinkled with blue cheese, complete this meal with a tossed green salad topped with blue cheese dressing!

Chicken Pot Roast Dinner

Prep Time: 10 Minutes • **Start to Finish: 8 Hours 25 Minutes** • **6 servings (1½ cups each)**

1 lb small unpeeled red potatoes (6 to 8), cut into 1-inch pieces (3 cups)

2 cups ready-to-eat baby-cut carrots

1 cup frozen small whole onions, thawed

6 boneless skinless chicken thighs (about 1¼ lb)

½ teaspoon salt

⅛ teaspoon pepper

1 jar (12 oz) chicken gravy

1½ cups frozen sweet peas, thawed

1 Spray 3½- to 4-quart slow cooker with cooking spray. In slow cooker, place potatoes, carrots and onions. Place chicken over vegetables; sprinkle with salt and pepper. Pour gravy over top.

2 Cover; cook on Low heat setting 8 to 10 hours.

3 Increase heat setting to High. Stir in peas. Cover; cook about 15 minutes or until peas are tender.

1 Serving: Calories 310; Total Fat 11g (Saturated Fat 3g, Trans Fat 0g); Cholesterol 60mg; Sodium 630mg; Total Carbohydrate 28g (Dietary Fiber 4g); Protein 24g **Exchanges:** 1½ Starch, 1½ Vegetable, 2½ Lean Meat, ½ Fat **Carbohydrate Choices:** 2

Make It a Meal
This is a great one-dish meal, but a fresh green salad is a nice addition to the meal. Choose baby greens and top with a favorite dressing.

Chicken Taco Chowder

Prep Time: 20 Minutes • Start to Finish: 5 Hours 35 Minutes • 8 servings

CHOWDER

- 4 cups diced Yukon Gold potatoes (about 3 medium)
- 3 cups frozen whole kernel corn
- 1 can (14.5 oz) fire-roasted diced tomatoes, drained
- 2 cans (4.5 oz each) chopped green chiles
- 1 medium onion, chopped (1 cup)
- 1 carton (32 oz) chicken broth (4 cups)
- 6 boneless skinless chicken thighs, cut into bite-size pieces
- 1 package (1 oz) taco seasoning mix
- ½ teaspoon ground red pepper (cayenne)
- 1 cup whipping cream
- 3 tablespoons cornstarch
- 3 tablespoons water
- 3 cups shredded Cheddar cheese (12 oz)

TOPPINGS, IF DESIRED

Shredded Cheddar cheese

Sour cream

Sliced green onions

1 Spray 5- to 6-quart slow cooker with cooking spray. In slow cooker, mix potatoes, corn, tomatoes, green chiles and onion. Stir in broth, chicken, taco seasoning mix and red pepper.

2 Cover; cook on Low heat setting 5 to 6 hours or until potatoes are tender.

3 Increase heat setting to High; stir in whipping cream. In small bowl, beat cornstarch and water. Beat cornstarch mixture into soup. Cover; cook about 15 minutes or until bubbly and thickened.

4 Add 3 cups Cheddar cheese to slow cooker; stir until melted. Serve soup with toppings.

1 Serving: Calories 530; Total Fat 29g (Saturated Fat 16g, Trans Fat 1g); Cholesterol 155mg; Sodium 1160mg; Total Carbohydrate 37g (Dietary Fiber 3g); Protein 30g **Exchanges:** 2 Starch, 1 Vegetable, 2 Lean Meat, 1 High-Fat Meat, 3 Fat **Carbohydrate Choices:** 2½

Customize It Crushed tortilla chips also make a nice garnish to this hearty chowder.

Genius Tip Yukon Gold potatoes have a waxy texture that holds up better than russet or baking potatoes, which tend to fall apart in the slow-cooking process.

Lemon-Pepper Chicken

Prep Time: 30 Minutes • Start to Finish: 4 Hours • 8 servings

3 tablespoons butter

8 bone-in skin-on chicken thighs (2½ to 3 lb)

1 teaspoon lemon-pepper seasoning

½ teaspoon salt

2 teaspoons finely chopped garlic

1 cup chicken broth (from 32-oz carton)

2 teaspoons grated lemon peel

2 tablespoons lemon juice

2 tablespoons cold water

2 tablespoons cornstarch

Cooked white rice, if desired

1 Spray 3½- to 4-quart slow cooker with cooking spray. In 12-inch nonstick skillet, heat 1 tablespoon of the butter over medium-high heat. Sprinkle chicken with ½ teaspoon of the lemon-pepper seasoning and the salt. Place half of the chicken thighs, skin side down, in skillet; cook 4 to 5 minutes or until skin is golden brown and chicken releases easily from surface. Turn chicken over; cook 2 minutes. Repeat for remaining chicken.

2 Layer chicken thighs, skin side up, inside slow cooker; sprinkle with garlic. In 2-cup measuring cup, mix chicken broth, lemon peel, lemon juice and remaining ½ teaspoon lemon-pepper seasoning; pour over chicken thighs.

3 Cover; cook on Low heat setting 3 to 3½ hours or until chicken is tender and juice is clear when thickest part is cut to bone (at least 165°F).

4 Remove chicken; place on serving platter and cover to keep warm. In small bowl, mix water and cornstarch; beat with whisk into cooking juices in slow cooker.

5 Cover; cook on High heat setting 20 to 30 minutes or until slightly thickened and bubbly around edges. Stir in remaining 2 tablespoons butter. Serve sauce with chicken and cooked rice.

1 Serving: Calories 240; Total Fat 15g (Saturated Fat 6g, Trans Fat 0g); Cholesterol 85mg; Sodium 410mg; Total Carbohydrate 3g (Dietary Fiber 0g); Protein 23g **Exchanges:** 3½ Lean Meat, 1 Fat **Carbohydrate Choices:** 0

Genius Tip If desired, garnish with fresh slices of lemon or chopped fresh Italian (flat-leaf) parsley.

Make It a Meal Add a green vegetable side such as broccoli florets or whole green beans to complete the meal.

Cheesy Chicken Spaghetti

Prep Time: 30 Minutes • Start to Finish: 2 Hours 30 Minutes • 8 servings

1 tablespoon butter, melted

1 tablespoon Worcestershire sauce

2 teaspoons seasoned salt

3 cloves garlic, finely chopped

1 package (20 oz) boneless skinless chicken thighs

1 can (28 oz) fire-roasted diced tomatoes, drained

1 can (18 oz) creamy mushroom soup

1 can (4.5 oz) chopped green chiles

1 package (8 oz) cream cheese, softened, cubed

2 cups shredded sharp Cheddar cheese (8 oz)

8 oz uncooked spaghetti

2 tablespoons chopped fresh Italian (flat-leaf) parsley

1 Spray 4- to 5-quart slow cooker with cooking spray. In large bowl, mix melted butter, Worcestershire sauce, seasoned salt and garlic. Add chicken; toss to coat. Pour mixture into slow cooker. In same bowl, mix tomatoes, soup and chiles; pour over chicken.

2 Cover; cook on High heat setting 2 to 3 hours (or Low heat setting 3 to 4 hours) or until thermometer inserted in thickest part of chicken reads at least 165°F.

3 Remove chicken from slow cooker; place on cutting board. Let stand 5 minutes or until cool enough to handle.

4 Add cream cheese and Cheddar cheese to mixture in slow cooker; stir to mix. Cover; cook on High heat setting 5 to 10 minutes or until cheese melts. Stir.

5 Meanwhile, cook spaghetti to desired doneness as directed on package. Drain. Shred chicken with 2 forks; return to slow cooker. Stir in cooked spaghetti. Top with parsley.

1 Serving: Calories 500; Total Fat 27g (Saturated Fat 14g, Trans Fat 0.5g); Cholesterol 135mg; Sodium 1110mg; Total Carbohydrate 34g (Dietary Fiber 2g); Protein 29g **Exchanges:** 1 Starch, 1 Other Carbohydrate, 1 Vegetable, 2½ Lean Meat, 1 High-Fat Meat, 2 Fat **Carbohydrate Choices:** 2

Genius Tip For ultimate creaminess, make sure cream cheese is completely soft before adding to the chicken mixture.

Buffalo Chicken Rigatoni

Prep Time: 25 Minutes • **Start to Finish: 2 Hours 45 Minutes** • **6 servings**

8 boneless skinless chicken thighs

½ teaspoon celery salt

¼ teaspoon salt

¼ teaspoon pepper

⅓ cup Buffalo wing sauce

2 cloves garlic, finely chopped

12 oz uncooked rigatoni

1 package (8 oz) cream cheese, softened, cubed

1½ cups shredded Cheddar cheese (6 oz)

⅓ cup blue cheese crumbles

⅓ cup thinly sliced green onions

1 Spray 4- or 5-quart slow cooker with cooking spray. Sprinkle chicken with celery salt, salt and pepper; place in slow cooker. Pour Buffalo sauce over chicken; stir in garlic.

2 Cover; cook on High heat setting 2 to 3 hours or until thermometer inserted in thickest part of chicken reads at least 165°F. Remove chicken; place on cutting board. Cool slightly.

3 Meanwhile, cook rigatoni as directed on package. Drain. Shred chicken, using 2 forks.

4 Stir in cream cheese and Cheddar cheese to mixture in slow cooker. Cover; cook 15 minutes. Beat with whisk until cheeses have melted into sauce. Stir in rigatoni and shredded chicken. Cover; cook about 5 minutes or until hot. Garnish with blue cheese and green onions.

1 Serving: Calories 690; Total Fat 33g (Saturated Fat 17g, Trans Fat 1g); Cholesterol 200mg; Sodium 1130mg; Total Carbohydrate 52g (Dietary Fiber 3g); Protein 46g **Exchanges:** 2 Starch, 1½ Other Carbohydrate, 4 Very Lean Meat, 1½ High-Fat Meat, 3½ Fat **Carbohydrate Choices:** 3½

Genius Tip Make sure to use Buffalo wing sauce rather than hot sauce in this recipe. The wing sauce has a buttery flavor and is milder than many hot sauces.

Customize It Blue cheese dressing is a traditional dip for Buffalo wings, which is why we use blue cheese as a garnish for this dish. It can be a strong flavor, though, so if you don't know your diner's preference, consider serving it on the side.

Mexican Honey-Garlic Chicken and Potatoes

Prep Time: 30 Minutes • Start to Finish: 3 Hours 30 Minutes • 6 servings

½ cup honey

1 package (0.85 oz) chicken taco seasoning mix

6 cloves garlic, finely chopped

1 tablespoon butter, melted

½ teaspoon salt

2 lb red potatoes, cut into ¾-inch pieces

1 package (2 lb) chicken legs (about 6)

1 lime, cut into wedges

2 green onions, thinly sliced

2 tablespoons chopped fresh cilantro

1 Spray 5- to 6-quart slow cooker with cooking spray. In large bowl, mix honey, taco seasoning mix, garlic, melted butter and salt. Add potatoes; toss to coat. Using slotted spoon, transfer potatoes to slow cooker. Add chicken to bowl with honey mixture; toss to coat. Arrange chicken on top of potatoes in slow cooker. Pour any remaining liquid over chicken.

2 Cover; cook on High heat setting 3 to 4 hours or until potatoes are tender and thermometer inserted in thickest part of chicken, without touching bone, reads at least 165°F. Do not uncover slow cooker before 3 hours.

3 Line 18×13-inch half-sheet pan with foil. Position oven rack 4 inches from broiling element. Set oven control to broil. Place chicken on pan. With slotted spoon, transfer potatoes to serving platter; cover with foil. Pour ¼ cup of liquid from slow cooker over chicken.

4 Broil 2 to 4 minutes or until chicken skin is golden brown and crisp. Turn chicken; pour another ¼ cup liquid from slow cooker over chicken. Discard remaining liquid from slow cooker. Broil 2 to 4 minutes longer or until skin is golden brown and crisp on second side.

5 Serve broiled chicken with sauce from pan, potatoes and lime wedges. Top with green onions and cilantro.

1 Serving: Calories 440; Total Fat 9g (Saturated Fat 3.5g, Trans Fat 0g); Cholesterol 150mg; Sodium 620mg; Total Carbohydrate 54g (Dietary Fiber 3g); Protein 35g **Exchanges:** 2 Starch, 1½ Other Carbohydrate, 4 Very Lean Meat, 1 Fat **Carbohydrate Choices:** 3½

Genius Tip To easily measure honey, spray a measuring cup with cooking spray before adding honey. The sticky stuff will slide right into your mixing bowl!

Genius Tip Wait until the last minute to chop the cilantro. The tender leaves wilt quickly once cut. To save a little time (and an extra cutting board), use kitchen scissors to snip cilantro directly over the finished dish.

Chicken Tortilla Soup

Prep Time: 15 Minutes • Start to Finish: 4 Hours 45 Minutes • 8 servings (1¼ cups each)

1 tablespoon vegetable oil

1 lb boneless skinless chicken breasts

¾ teaspoon salt

½ teaspoon pepper

2 cups water

1½ cups chicken broth (from 32-oz carton)

1 can (14.5 oz) fire-roasted diced tomatoes, undrained

1 can (11 oz) whole kernel corn, red and green peppers, drained

1 can (10 oz) enchilada sauce

1 large onion, chopped (1 cup)

1 can (4.5 oz) chopped green chiles

1 teaspoon ground cumin

1 teaspoon chili powder

½ cup chopped fresh cilantro

4 cups coarsely crushed tortilla chips

½ cup sour cream

1 Spray 5- to 6-quart slow cooker with cooking spray. In 12-inch nonstick skillet, heat oil over medium-high heat. Add chicken to skillet; sprinkle with salt and pepper. Cook 4 minutes, turning once, until browned on both sides. Place chicken in slow cooker. Add water, broth, tomatoes, corn, enchilada sauce, onion, green chiles, cumin and chili powder.

2 Cover; cook on Low heat setting 4 hours or until chicken is tender.

3 Remove chicken from slow cooker; place on cutting board. Cool slightly. Shred chicken, using 2 forks. Return chicken to slow cooker. Stir in cilantro. Cover; cook 30 minutes. Top each serving with ½ cup crushed tortilla chips and 1 tablespoon sour cream.

1 Serving: Calories 290; Total Fat 11g (Saturated Fat 2g, Trans Fat 0g); Cholesterol 0mg; Sodium 1090mg; Total Carbohydrate 28g (Dietary Fiber 3g); Protein 17g **Exchanges:** 2 Starch, 1½ Very Lean Meat, 1½ Fat **Carbohydrate Choices:** 2

MAKE IT IN ONE

Cheesy Chicken Enchilada Chili

Prep Time: 10 Minutes • Start to Finish: 4 Hours 10 Minutes • 4 servings (1¼ cups each)

1 package (20 oz) boneless skinless chicken thighs, cut into 1-inch pieces

1 can (15.2 oz) whole kernel sweet corn, drained, rinsed

1 can (15 oz) black beans, drained, rinsed

1 can (10 oz) mild enchilada sauce

2 tablespoons taco seasoning mix (from 1-oz package)

2 cups shredded Colby–Monterey Jack cheese blend (8 oz)

Chopped green onions and sour cream, if desired

4 cups (about 5 oz) tortilla chips

1 Spray 3½- or 4-quart slow cooker with cooking spray. In slow cooker, mix chicken, corn, beans, enchilada sauce and taco seasoning mix. Cover and cook on Low heat setting 8 hours or High heat setting 4 hours.

2 Stir in 1 cup of the cheese. Top with green onions and sour cream. Top with remaining cheese; serve with tortilla chips.

1 Serving: Calories 710; Total Fat 33g (Saturated Fat 14g, Trans Fat 0.5g); Cholesterol 190mg; Sodium 1640mg; Total Carbohydrate 52g (Dietary Fiber 6g); Protein 51g **Exchanges:** 2½ Starch, 1 Other Carbohydrate, ½ Very Lean Meat, 4 Lean Meat, 2 High-Fat Meat, ½ Fat **Carbohydrate Choices:** 3½

Customize It Try shredded 4-cheese Mexican cheese blend instead of the Colby–Monterey Jack.

Customize It Why not turn this into nachos? Use a slotted spoon to top the chips with the chili. Instead of stirring in cheese, sprinkle it all on top at the end.

Classic Meat Loaf

Prep Time: 20 Minutes • Start to Finish: 3 Hours 20 Minutes • 6 servings

1½ lb lean (at least 80%) ground beef

1 cup milk

1 teaspoon chopped fresh sage leaves or ¼ teaspoon dried sage leaves

½ teaspoon salt

½ teaspoon ground mustard

¼ teaspoon pepper

1 clove garlic, finely chopped, or ⅛ teaspoon garlic powder

1 egg

3 slices bread, torn into small pieces

1 small onion, chopped (¼ cup)

½ cup ketchup

1 Line 4½- to 5-quart slow cooker with foil. Spray foil with cooking spray. In large bowl, mix all ingredients except ketchup. Shape mixture into loaf; place in center of slow cooker. Spread ketchup over top.

2 Cover; cook on Low heat setting 3 to 4 hours or until meat thermometer inserted in center of loaf reads 160°F.

3 Remove meat loaf from slow cooker; place on serving platter. Cut into pieces to serve.

1 Serving: Calories 290; Total Fat 15g (Saturated Fat 6g, Trans Fat 1g); Cholesterol 105mg; Sodium 560mg; Total Carbohydrate 15g (Dietary Fiber 0g); Protein 24g **Exchanges:** ½ Starch, ½ Other Carbohydrate, 3½ Lean Meat, 1 Fat **Carbohydrate Choices:** 1

Genius Tip To make ahead, prepare and shape the meat loaf in advance; cover and refrigerate up to 5 hours. Place in slow cooker and cook as directed.

Burgundy Stew with Herb Dumplings

Prep Time: 25 Minutes • **Start to Finish: 8 Hours 50 Minutes** • **8 servings**

STEW

2 lb boneless beef bottom or top round, tip or chuck steak, cut into 1-inch pieces

4 medium carrots, cut into ¼-inch slices (2 cups)

2 medium stalks celery, sliced (⅔ cup)

2 medium onions, sliced

1 can (14.5 oz) diced tomatoes, undrained

1 can (8 oz) sliced mushrooms, drained

¾ cup dry red wine or beef broth

1½ teaspoons salt

1 teaspoon dried thyme leaves

1 teaspoon ground mustard

¼ teaspoon pepper

¼ cup water

3 tablespoons all-purpose flour

DUMPLINGS

1½ cups Original Bisquick® Mix

½ teaspoon dried thyme leaves

¼ teaspoon dried sage leaves, crumbled

½ cup milk

1 Spray 5- to 6-quart slow cooker with cooking spray. In slow cooker, mix all stew ingredients except water and flour.

2 Cover; cook on Low heat setting 8 to 10 hours (or High heat setting 4 to 5 hours) or until beef is tender.

3 In small bowl, stir water and flour until well mixed; gradually stir into beef mixture. Cover.

4 In medium bowl, mix dumpling ingredients just until moistened. Drop dough by 8 spoonfuls onto hot beef mixture. If using Low heat setting, increase to High.

5 Cover; cook 25 to 35 minutes or until toothpick inserted in center of dumplings comes out clean.

1 Serving: Calories 300; Total Fat 7g (Saturated Fat 2.5g, Trans Fat 0g); Cholesterol 75mg; Sodium 830mg; Total Carbohydrate 28g (Dietary Fiber 3g); Protein 32g **Exchanges:** 1½ Starch, 1 Vegetable, 3½ Very Lean Meat, 1 Fat **Carbohydrate Choices:** 2

Make It a Meal

Make It a Meal Just a crisp salad on the side is all you need to round out this delicious hearty meal.

Swiss Steak with Carrots and Potatoes

Prep Time: 15 Minutes • Start to Finish: 7 Hours 15 Minutes • 6 servings

1½ lb boneless beef round steak

½ teaspoon peppered seasoned salt

6 to 8 small red potatoes, cut into quarters

1½ cups ready-to-eat baby-cut carrots

1 medium onion, sliced

1 can (14.5 oz) diced tomatoes with Italian herbs, undrained

1 jar (12 oz) beef gravy

Chopped fresh parsley, if desired

1 Spray 4- to 5-quart slow cooker with cooking spray. Cut beef into 6 serving pieces. Spray 12-inch skillet with cooking spray; heat over medium-high heat. Sprinkle beef with seasoned salt. Cook in skillet 6 to 8 minutes, turning once, until brown.

2 In slow cooker, layer potatoes, carrots, beef and onion. In medium bowl, mix tomatoes and gravy; spoon over mixture in slow cooker.

3 Cover; cook on Low heat setting 7 to 8 hours. Sprinkle with parsley.

1 Serving: Calories 260; Total Fat 6g (Saturated Fat 2g, Trans Fat 0g); Cholesterol 75mg; Sodium 620mg; Total Carbohydrate 21g (Dietary Fiber 3g); Protein 32g **Exchanges:** 1 Starch, 1 Vegetable, 3 Very Lean Meat, 1 Lean Meat **Carbohydrate Choices:** 1½

Genius Tip Leaving the peel on the potatoes not only retains nutrients but also helps potatoes keep their shape. Just clean and cut as directed.

Customize It Peppered seasoned salt is one of the newest varieties of seasoned salt available in the supermarket. If you can't find it, use regular seasoned salt and sprinkle the beef with pepper, or you can just use salt and pepper.

Fire-Roasted Tomato Pot Roast

Prep Time: 15 Minutes • Start to Finish: 4 Hours 15 Minutes • 6 servings

1 large onion, halved, thinly sliced

1 lb small red potatoes, cut into quarters

1 bag (12 oz) ready-to-eat baby-cut carrots

1 tablespoon chopped garlic

1 boneless beef chuck roast (2½ to 3 lb), trimmed of excess fat

1 teaspoon salt

½ teaspoon pepper

1 can (14.5 oz) fire-roasted crushed tomatoes, undrained

Chopped fresh parsley, if desired

1 Spray 5- to 6-quart slow cooker with cooking spray. Arrange onion, potatoes, carrots and garlic in bottom of slow cooker.

2 Place beef over vegetables. Sprinkle with salt and pepper. Pour tomatoes over beef and vegetables.

3 Cover; cook on Low heat setting 6 to 8 hours (or High heat setting 4 to 5 hours) or until beef is tender. Serve beef and vegetables with sauce. Garnish with parsley.

1 Serving: Calories 430; Total Fat 20g (Saturated Fat 8g, Trans Fat 1g); Cholesterol 120mg; Sodium 620mg; Total Carbohydrate 25g (Dietary Fiber 4g); Protein 37g **Exchanges:** 1 Starch, ½ Other Carbohydrate, 1 Vegetable, 4½ Lean Meat, 1 Fat **Carbohydrate Choices:** 1½

Genius Tip Resist the urge to open up the slow cooker. You will get best results if you keep it closed.

Genius Tip Trimming away excess fat from your beef roast before cooking helps to make the sauce less fatty.

Barbecue Beef Sandwiches

Prep Time: 20 Minutes • Start to Finish: 7 Hours 40 Minutes • 12 sandwiches

1 boneless beef chuck roast (3 lb), trimmed of excess fat

1 cup barbecue sauce

½ cup peach or apricot preserves

⅓ cup chopped green bell pepper

1 tablespoon Dijon mustard

2 teaspoons packed brown sugar

1 small onion, sliced

12 kaiser or hamburger buns, split

1 Spray 4- to 5-quart slow cooker with cooking spray. Cut beef into 4 pieces. Place beef in slow cooker. In medium bowl, mix all remaining ingredients except buns; pour over beef.

2 Cover; cook on Low heat setting 7 to 8 hours or until beef is tender.

3 Remove beef from cooker; place on cutting board. Cut into thin slices; return to cooker.

4 Cover; cook on Low heat setting 20 to 30 minutes longer or until beef is hot. Fill buns with beef mixture.

1 Sandwich: Calories 410; Total Fat 14g (Saturated Fat 5g, Trans Fat 1g); Cholesterol 60g; Sodium 570mg; Total Carbohydrate 46g (Dietary Fiber 1g); Protein 26g **Exchanges:** 1½ Starch, 1½ Other Carbohydrate, 3 Lean Meat, 1 Fat **Carbohydrate Choices:** 3

Customize It For a delicious kick, spread buns with horseradish sauce.

Customize It To make each bite extra delicious, serve the leftover cooker juices in small bowls and dip the sandwiches into the juices!

Mexican Pot Roast

Prep Time: 15 Minutes • Start to Finish: 8 Hours 15 Minutes • 6 servings

1   large onion, halved, thinly sliced

1   lb baby red potatoes (about 8 potatoes)

1   boneless beef chuck roast (2½ to 3 lb), trimmed of excess fat

1   package (1 oz) taco seasoning mix

2   teaspoons ground cumin

½   teaspoon ground red pepper (cayenne)

½   teaspoon salt

½   teaspoon pepper

1   can (14.5 oz) fire-roasted diced tomatoes, drained

1 Spray 5- to 6-quart slow cooker with cooking spray. Arrange onion and potatoes in slow cooker. Place beef over vegetables. Sprinkle with taco seasoning mix, cumin, red pepper, salt and pepper. Pour tomatoes over beef and vegetables.

2 Cover; cook on Low heat setting 8 to 9 hours or until beef is tender. Serve beef and vegetables with sauce.

1 Serving: Calories 410; Total Fat 20g (Saturated Fat 8g, Trans Fat 1g); Cholesterol 105mg; Sodium 650mg; Total Carbohydrate 21g (Dietary Fiber 2g); Protein 37g **Exchanges:** 1 Starch, ½ Vegetable, 5 Lean Meat, 1 Fat **Carbohydrate Choices:** 1½

Genius Tip Keeping the baby red potatoes whole helps to prevent them from falling apart and getting too soft during the long cooking process.

Genius Tip Because slow cookers are sealed units that don't allow for any liquid evaporation, it's important to thoroughly drain the canned tomatoes to ensure the pot roast doesn't become too watery.

Red Wine Beef and Blue Cheese Sandwiches

Prep Time: 15 Minutes • Start to Finish: 7 Hours 15 Minutes • 10 servings (1 sandwich)

1 boneless beef chuck roast (3 lb)

1 teaspoon salt

1 medium onion, thinly sliced

1 teaspoon dried rosemary leaves

1 teaspoon dried thyme leaves

1 clove garlic, finely chopped

1 dried bay leaf

3 or 4 black peppercorns

1 cup dry red wine or nonalcoholic red wine

¾ cup beef-flavored broth (from 32-oz carton)

1 teaspoon Worcestershire sauce

10 soft ciabatta rolls or hoagie buns, split, toasted if desired

1¼ cups crumbled Stilton or blue cheese (5 oz)

1 Spray 3½- to 4-quart slow cooker with cooking spray. Sprinkle beef with salt (if roast comes in netting or is tied, do not remove). Place beef and onion in slow cooker. In small bowl, mix rosemary, thyme, garlic, bay leaf, peppercorns, wine, broth and Worcestershire sauce; pour over beef.

2 Cover; cook on Low heat setting 7 to 8 hours.

3 Skim fat from surface of cooking liquid; discard bay leaf and peppercorns. Remove beef from slow cooker to cutting board (remove netting or strings). Cut beef into thin slices. Serve beef in rolls topped with onions and cheese. Serve with broth from slow cooker for dipping.

1 Serving: Calories 560; Total Fat 23g (Saturated Fat 10g, Trans Fat 1.5g); Cholesterol 90mg; Sodium 990mg; Total Carbohydrate 49g (Dietary Fiber 2g); Protein 39g **Exchanges:** 3 Starch, ½ Other Carbohydrate, 3 Lean Meat, 1 Medium-Fat Meat, 1½ Fat **Carbohydrate Choices:** 3

Customize It Substitute mozzarella cheese for the Stilton and serve on French rolls.

Salisbury Steak Meatballs

Prep Time: 30 Minutes • Start to Finish: 3 Hours 40 Minutes • 8 servings

MEATBALLS

- 2 tablespoons butter, melted
- 1 tablespoon tomato paste
- ½ teaspoon salt
- 2 cups thinly sliced onions
- 8 oz mushrooms, thinly sliced (about 3 cups)
- 1 cup beef broth (from 32-oz carton)
- 1 lb lean (at least 80%) ground beef
- ½ cup plain panko crispy bread crumbs
- ⅓ cup milk
- 1 egg, slightly beaten
- 1 tablespoon Montreal steak grill seasoning
- 1 tablespoon soy sauce
- 2 tablespoons cornstarch
- 2 tablespoons cold water

POTATOES

- 1 pouch (4.7 oz) creamy butter mashed potatoes
- 2 tablespoons chopped fresh Italian (flat-leaf) parsley

1 Spray 5- or 6-quart slow cooker with cooking spray. Mix melted butter, tomato paste and salt in slow cooker. Add onions and mushrooms; toss to coat. Stir in broth.

2 In large bowl, mix beef, bread crumbs, milk, egg, grill seasoning and soy sauce. Shape into about 24 (1½-inch) meatballs. Place meatballs in slow cooker on top of vegetable mixture.

3 Cover; cook on Low heat setting 3 to 4 hours or until meatballs are thoroughly cooked (165°F). Stir. In small bowl, beat cornstarch and cold water. Quickly stir into slow cooker; cover. Increase to High heat setting; cook 5 to 10 minutes or until thickened.

4 Make mashed potatoes as directed on package. Serve meatballs over mashed potatoes. Sprinkle with parsley.

1 Serving: Calories 280; Total Fat 13g (Saturated Fat 5g, Trans Fat 0g); Cholesterol 70mg; Sodium 1030mg; Total Carbohydrate 26g (Dietary Fiber 1g); Protein 15g **Exchanges:** 1 Starch, ½ Other Carbohydrate, 1 Vegetable, 1½ Lean Meat, 1½ Fat **Carbohydrate Choices:** 2

Customize It A simple pouch of mashed potatoes really makes these easy slow-cooker meatballs into a meal. We liked the creamy butter flavor with the meatballs, but the roasted garlic flavor would be great, too.

Asian-Style Beef Roast with Rice

Prep Time: 30 Minutes • **Start to Finish:** 8 Hours 30 Minutes • **8 servings**

BEEF

1 cup beef broth (from 32-oz carton)

¼ cup packed brown sugar

¼ cup soy sauce

2 tablespoons chili garlic sauce

½ teaspoon ground gingerroot

6 green onions, sliced, white and green parts separated

1 boneless beef chuck roast (2 to 3 lb), trimmed of excess fat

¼ cup cornstarch

¼ cup cold water

RICE AND GARNISH

4 cups hot cooked white rice

¼ cup chopped fresh cilantro

1 tablespoon toasted sesame seed

1 lime, cut into wedges

1 Spray 3½- or 4-quart slow cooker with cooking spray. Place broth, brown sugar, soy sauce, chili garlic sauce and gingerroot in slow cooker; stir with whisk to combine. Stir in green onion whites. Add beef to slow cooker; turn to coat.

2 Cover; cook on Low heat setting 8 to 9 hours or until very tender.

3 Remove roast from cooker; place on cutting board. Cool slightly. Slice thinly or shred beef, using 2 forks. Return beef to mixture in slow cooker. Increase to High heat setting. In small bowl, beat cornstarch and cold water. Quickly stir into liquid mixture in slow cooker. Cover; cook 5 to 10 minutes or until thickened.

4 Divide rice among 8 bowls. Divide shredded beef among bowls of rice. Top with reserved green onion greens, cilantro and sesame seed; serve with lime wedges.

1 Serving: Calories 360; Total Fat 13g (Saturated Fat 5g, Trans Fat 0.5g); Cholesterol 60mg; Sodium 950mg; Total Carbohydrate 36g (Dietary Fiber 1g); Protein 24g **Exchanges:** 1½ Starch, 1 Other Carbohydrate, 3 Lean Meat, ½ Fat **Carbohydrate Choices:** 2½

Make It a Meal Serve with steamed, salted edamame to round out this Japanese-inspired meal.

Genius Tip Keep microwavable frozen cooked rice on hand to shave off a few more precious predinner minutes.

Italian Pork Loin with Beans and Tomatoes

Prep Time: 30 Minutes • **Start to Finish: 3 Hours 35 Minutes** • **8 servings**

2 cans (15 oz each) cannellini beans, drained, rinsed

1 cup thinly sliced onion

1 red bell pepper, cut into thin slices

1 tablespoon Italian seasoning

2 tablespoons vegetable oil

2 teaspoons salt

1 boneless pork loin roast (2½ to 3½ lb), trimmed of excess fat

1 can (28 oz) fire-roasted diced tomatoes, drained

1 cup shredded mozzarella cheese (4 oz)

¼ cup shredded fresh basil leaves

1 Spray 5- to 6-quart slow cooker with cooking spray. Mix beans, onions, bell pepper, Italian seasoning, 1 tablespoon of the oil and 1 teaspoon of the salt in slow cooker.

2 Rub pork loin with remaining 1 tablespoon oil and remaining 1 teaspoon salt. Heat 12-inch nonstick skillet over medium-high heat. Cook pork in hot skillet 3 to 5 minutes on both sides or until browned. Place roast in slow cooker. Pour tomatoes over pork.

3 Cover; cook on Low heat setting 3 to 4 hours or until pork is thoroughly cooked and thermometer inserted in center reads 145°F.

4 Place pork on cutting board; let stand until cool enough to handle. Stir bean mixture in slow cooker. Using slotted spoon, transfer to serving platter. Cut pork into 8 slices; place on top of bean mixture on platter. Top with mozzarella cheese. Cover platter with foil for 3 to 5 minutes or until cheese melts. Remove foil; top with basil.

1 Serving: Calories 390; Total Fat 17g (Saturated Fat 6g, Trans Fat 0g); Cholesterol 100mg; Sodium 1060mg; Total Carbohydrate 19g (Dietary Fiber 5g); Protein 40g **Exchanges:** ½ Starch, ½ Other Carbohydrate, 1 Vegetable, 5 Lean Meat, ½ Medium-Fat Meat **Carbohydrate Choices:** 1

Genius Tip Pork loin roasts often come with a thin layer of fat on one side. Trim it off before cooking, or ask your butcher to remove it for you.

Genius Tip The bean mixture in the slow cooker will be brothy. The broth is very flavorful, but if you prefer less liquid, use a colander instead of a slotted spoon to drain the bean mixture.

Pulled Pork Stew with Corn

Prep Time: 20 Minutes • **Start to Finish: 9 Hours 50 Minutes** • **12 servings**

STEW

- 1 can (19 oz) red enchilada sauce
- 1 package (1 oz) taco seasoning mix
- 2 tablespoons chili powder
- 2 teaspoons dried oregano leaves
- 2 teaspoons ground cumin
- 2 teaspoons salt
- 1 boneless pork shoulder roast (3 to 4 lb)
- 1 carton (32 oz) chicken broth
- 1 can (28 oz) fire-roasted crushed tomatoes, undrained
- 1 can (15.25 oz) whole kernel corn, drained

TOPPINGS, IF DESIRED

- Sliced radishes
- Shredded cabbage
- Diced avocado
- Crumbled queso fresco
- Chopped fresh cilantro
- Lime wedges

1 Spray 5- to 6-quart slow cooker with cooking spray. Mix enchilada sauce, taco seasoning mix, chili powder, oregano, cumin and salt in slow cooker. Add pork; turn to coat.

2 Cover; cook on Low heat setting 8 to 9 hours or until very tender. Remove pork from slow cooker; place on cutting board. When cool enough to handle, shred pork, using 2 forks. Remove 1 cup cooking liquid; place in large bowl. Add shredded pork to bowl; toss to coat.

3 Meanwhile, discard remaining cooking liquid; carefully wipe out slow cooker with paper towel. Spray slow cooker with cooking spray. Add broth, tomatoes and corn; stir in pork.

4 Cover; cook on High heat setting 1 hour 30 minutes to 2 hours 30 minutes or until hot. Serve with toppings.

1 Serving: Calories 290; Total Fat 17g (Saturated Fat 6g, Trans Fat 0g); Cholesterol 75mg; Sodium 1260mg; Total Carbohydrate 14g (Dietary Fiber 1g); Protein 21g **Exchanges:** ½ Other Carbohydrate, 1 Vegetable, 2½ Lean Meat, 2 Fat **Carbohydrate Choices:** 1

Customize It Want to save time after shredding pork? Instead of heating broth mixture in slow cooker, place broth, tomatoes and corn in large microwavable bowl. Cover with plastic wrap, and microwave on High 8 to 10 minutes or until steaming. Pour into clean slow cooker, stir in pork and keep warm until ready to serve.

Genius Tip Place pork, fatty side up, in slow cooker so roast bastes itself as it cooks.

Barbecue Pulled-Pork Fajitas

Prep Time: 15 Minutes • Start to Finish: 10 Hours 30 Minutes • 18 fajitas

1 boneless pork loin roast (2½ lb), trimmed of excess fat

1 medium onion, thinly sliced

2 cups barbecue sauce

¾ cup chunky-style salsa

1 tablespoon chili powder

1 teaspoon ground cumin

1 bag (1 lb) frozen stir-fry bell peppers and onions

½ teaspoon salt

18 flour tortillas (8 inch)

Shredded cheese, if desired

Guacamole, if desired

Sour cream, if desired

1 Spray 3½- to 4-quart slow cooker with cooking spray. Place pork in slow cooker. Place onion on top. In small bowl, mix barbecue sauce, salsa, chili powder and cumin; pour over pork and onion.

2 Cover and cook on Low heat setting 8 to 10 hours.

3 Remove pork from cooker; place on cutting board. Shred pork, using 2 forks. Return pork to cooker; mix well. Stir in stir-fry vegetables and salt.

4 Increase heat setting to High. Cover and cook 30 minutes or until mixture is hot and vegetables are tender.

5 Using slotted spoon, fill each tortilla with ½ cup pork mixture. Fold 1 end of tortilla up about 1 inch over filling; fold right and left sides over folded end, overlapping. Fold remaining end down. Serve with cheese, guacamole and sour cream.

1 Fajita: Calories 320; Total Fat 9g (Saturated Fat 3g, Trans Fat 0g); Cholesterol 40mg; Sodium 850mg; Total Carbohydrate 40g (Dietary Fiber 3g); Protein 18g **Exchanges:** 1 Starch, 1½ Other Carbohydrate, ½ Vegetable, 2 Lean Meat, ½ Fat **Carbohydrate Choices:** 2½

Genius Tip
Leftover shredded pork can be stored in the refrigerator for up to 4 days or frozen up to 4 months.

Cheesy Bacon-Ranch Potato Soup

Prep Time: 30 Minutes • Start to Finish: 5 Hours 45 Minutes • 6 servings

6 slices bacon

1 medium onion, chopped (1 cup)

1 carton (32 oz) reduced-sodium chicken broth (4 cups)

3 medium Yukon Gold potatoes, diced

1 package (1 oz) ranch dressing and seasoning mix

1 cup whipping cream

2 tablespoons cornstarch

2 tablespoons water

1 loaf (8 oz) prepared cheese product, cut into cubes

2 cups shredded sharp Cheddar cheese (8 oz)

1 Spray 5- to 6-quart slow cooker with cooking spray. Heat 12-inch skillet over medium heat. Cook bacon in skillet 10 to 15 minutes or until crisp. Place on paper towels to drain. Reserve 1 tablespoon drippings in skillet. Crumble 3 slices of the bacon; cover and refrigerate until ready to serve. Crumble remaining 3 slices; place in slow cooker.

2 Add onion to drippings in skillet; cook 4 to 6 minutes, stirring occasionally, until tender. Place onion mixture in slow cooker. Stir in broth, potatoes and ranch dressing mix.

3 Cover; cook on Low heat setting 5 to 6 hours or until bubbly and potatoes are tender.

4 Increase heat setting to High; stir in whipping cream. In small bowl, beat cornstarch and water with whisk. Beat cornstarch mixture into soup. Cover; cook about 15 minutes or until slightly thickened.

5 Add cheese product to slow cooker; stir until melted. Add 1½ cups of the Cheddar cheese; stir until melted. Serve soup with remaining ½ cup Cheddar cheese and reserved crumbled bacon.

1 Serving: Calories 570; Total Fat 38g (Saturated Fat 22g, Trans Fat 1.5g); Cholesterol 135mg; Sodium 1640mg; Total Carbohydrate 32g (Dietary Fiber 2g); Protein 23g **Exchanges:** 1½ Starch, ½ Milk, ½ Vegetable, 1 Medium-Fat Meat, 1 High-Fat Meat, 4 Fat **Carbohydrate Choices:** 2

Customize It Cheddar cheese comes in a variety of types from mild to extra sharp. If you're looking for a less intense Cheddar flavor, use mild Cheddar. If you enjoy a more intense Cheddar flavor, use sharp Cheddar.

Genius Tip Yukon Gold potatoes have a waxy texture that holds up better than russet or baking potatoes, which tend to fall apart in the slow-cooking process.

Southwest Shredded Pork

Prep Time: 25 Minutes • **Start to Finish: 8 Hours 25 Minutes** • **12 servings**

PORK MIXTURE

- 1 can (28 oz) fire-roasted diced tomatoes, drained
- 1 can (15 oz) black beans, drained, rinsed
- 1 can (4.5 oz) chopped green chiles
- 2 cups chopped onions
- 1 medium red bell pepper, diced
- 2 packages (1 oz each) taco seasoning mix
- 1 boneless pork shoulder roast (3 to 4 lb)
- 6 cups hot cooked white rice

TOPPINGS, IF DESIRED

Shredded Colby–Monterey Jack cheese

Sour cream

Lime wedges

1 Spray 5- to 6-quart slow cooker with cooking spray. In slow cooker, mix tomatoes, beans, chiles, onions, bell pepper and taco seasoning mix. Add pork; turn to coat.

2 Cover; cook on Low heat setting 8 to 9 hours or until very tender.

3 Remove pork from slow cooker. When cool enough to handle, shred meat, using 2 forks. Stir shredded pork into mixture in slow cooker. Serve with rice and toppings.

1 Serving: Calories 370; Total Fat 13g (Saturated Fat 4.5g, Trans Fat 0g); Cholesterol 70mg; Sodium 860mg; Total Carbohydrate 35g (Dietary Fiber 2g), Protein 27g **Exchanges:** 2 Starch, 1 Vegetable, 2½ Lean Meat, 1 Fat **Carbohydrate Choices:** 2

Genius Tip To use the pork in enchiladas, quesadillas or sandwiches, just drain the liquid using a colander or slotted spoon.

Customize It Red kidney or pinto beans are both good substitutes for the black beans.

Pulled Pork Chili with Fire-Roasted Tomatoes

Prep Time: 20 Minutes • Start to Finish: 8 Hours 35 Minutes • 6 servings

CHILI

- 1 boneless pork shoulder roast (2½ lb), trimmed of excess fat, cut into 4-inch pieces
- 1 package (0.85 oz) chicken taco seasoning mix
- 1 can (15 oz) pinto beans, drained, rinsed
- 1 can (28 oz) fire-roasted crushed tomatoes, undrained
- 1 cup chicken broth (from 32-oz carton)
- 1 can (4.5 oz) chopped green chiles
- 1 medium onion, chopped
- 1 to 2 serrano chiles, seeds removed, finely chopped
- 2 cloves garlic, finely chopped

TOPPINGS, IF DESIRED

Shredded Cheddar cheese

Sour cream

Thinly sliced green onions

1 Spray 5- to 6-quart slow cooker with cooking spray. Place pork pieces in slow cooker; sprinkle taco seasoning mix over top and toss to coat. Add remaining chili ingredients to slow cooker; stir to combine.

2 Cover; cook on Low heat setting 8 to 9 hours or until pork is very tender.

3 Place pork on cutting board; shred pork, using 2 forks. Place shredded pork back into slow cooker; stir to combine. Cook on Low heat 15 minutes or until hot. Serve with toppings.

I Serving: Calories 480; Total Fat 22g (Saturated Fat 8g, Trans Fat 0g); Cholesterol 115mg; Sodium 910mg; Total Carbohydrate 26g (Dietary Fiber 4g); Protein 43g **Exchanges:** ½ Starch, 1 Other Carbohydrate, 1½ Vegetable, 5½ Lean Meat, 1 Fat **Carbohydrate Choices:** 2

Customize It If you're not sure how hot your crowd likes their chili, just use 1 serrano in the chili, and serve a small bowl of finely chopped fresh serranos on the side. That way, everyone can adjust the heat level to their own liking.

Customize It If you want to give a Mexican spin to this chili, consider adding fresh cilantro and limes wedges to your garnishes.

Skinny Spinach Lasagna

Prep Time: 30 Minutes • Start to Finish: 4 Hours 40 Minutes • 8 servings

1 jar (25.5 oz) tomato basil pasta sauce

1 can (14.5 oz) fire-roasted crushed or diced tomatoes, undrained

1/4 teaspoon crushed red pepper, if desired

1 yellow bell pepper, coarsely chopped

1 zucchini, halved and thinly sliced

9 uncooked lasagna noodles

1 1/4 cups light ricotta cheese

1 1/2 cups shredded part-skim mozzarella cheese (6 oz)

4 cups coarsely chopped fresh baby spinach (4 oz)

1 Spray 5- to 6-quart slow cooker with cooking spray. In medium bowl, mix pasta sauce, tomatoes, crushed red pepper, bell pepper and zucchini. Spread 1 cup tomato mixture in bottom of slow cooker.

2 Layer 3 lasagna noodles, broken into pieces to fit, over sauce in slow cooker. Spread half of the ricotta cheese over noodles; sprinkle with 1/4 cup of the mozzarella cheese and half of the spinach. Top with one-third of the tomato sauce mixture (about 1 1/2 cups). Repeat layering of noodles, cheeses and spinach. Top with remaining 3 noodles and sauce. Save remaining 1 cup mozzarella cheese in refrigerator.

3 Cover; cook on Low heat setting 4 to 5 hours or until noodles are tender and cooked through. Sprinkle with reserved mozzarella cheese; cover and let stand 10 minutes to melt cheese.

1 Serving: Calories 280; Total Fat 8g (Saturated Fat 4.5g, Trans Fat 0g); Cholesterol 25mg; Sodium 530mg; Total Carbohydrate 34g (Dietary Fiber 3g); Protein 16g **Exchanges:** 2 Starch, 1 Vegetable, 1 Lean Meat, 1 Fat **Carbohydrate Choices:** 2

Genius Tip You can make this recipe up to 24 hours ahead of time. Assemble the lasagna, cover tightly with foil and refrigerate in the slow-cooker insert. Cook time will take longer; cook until thoroughly heated in center.

Customize It Try other vegetables in the lasagna such as sliced mushrooms, sliced yellow summer squash, thinly sliced red onion, grated carrots or green bell pepper.

Chana Masala

Prep Time: 20 Minutes • Start to Finish: 4 Hours 20 Minutes • 6 servings

1 can (28 oz) crushed tomatoes, undrained

2 cans (19 oz each) chick peas (garbanzo beans), drained, rinsed

1 tablespoon olive oil

2 cups chopped onions (2 large)

½ teaspoon salt

1 jalapeño chile, diced

1 tablespoon grated gingerroot

2 tablespoons curry powder

2 teaspoons paprika

1 teaspoon garam masala

¼ teaspoon ground red pepper (cayenne)

1 lime, cut into 6 wedges

Hot cooked basmati rice or naan

1 Spray 3½- to 4-quart slow cooker with cooking spray. Place tomatoes and chick peas in slow cooker.

2 In 10-inch skillet, heat oil over medium heat. Add onions; cook until onions are tender. Add salt, jalapeño chile and gingerroot. Cook 1 minute. Stir in curry powder, paprika, garam masala and red pepper; cook until spices begin to brown. Add spice mixture to slow cooker. Add 3 tablespoons water to same skillet. Beat with whisk to remove all spices and browned bits left in pan; add to slow cooker. Stir well.

3 Cover; cook on Low heat setting 4 to 6 hours (or on High heat setting 2 to 3 hours).

4 Serve with lime wedges and rice.

1 Serving: Calories 280; Total Fat 7g (Saturated Fat 0.5g, Trans Fat 0g); Cholesterol 0mg; Sodium 680mg; Total Carbohydrate 44g (Dietary Fiber 12g); Protein 11g **Exchanges:** 1½ Starch, 1 Other Carbohydrate, 1½ Vegetable, ½ Very Lean Meat, 1 Fat **Carbohydrate Choices:** 3

Customize It Stir 3 cups baby spinach leaves into the Chana Masala after it is finished cooking. Cover; cook 10 minutes longer or until spinach is wilted.

Genius Tip Basmati is the traditional rice served with Chana Masala; however, feel free to use your favorite rice. If you are in a time crunch, look for bags of frozen cooked rice in the frozen vegetable section of your grocery store.

Spinach and Mushroom Tortellini

Prep Time: 30 Minutes • Start to Finish: 7 Hours 50 Minutes • 6 servings

- 1 package (8 oz) mushrooms, thinly sliced
- 1 cup thinly sliced onion
- 4 tablespoons butter, melted
- 2 tablespoons soy sauce
- ½ teaspoon salt
- ½ teaspoon pepper
- 2 cups vegetable broth (from 32-oz carton)
- 1 package (20 oz) refrigerated cheese-filled tortellini
- 1 package (8 oz) cream cheese, softened, cubed
- 3 cups baby spinach leaves, lightly packed
- ½ cup shredded Parmesan cheese (2 oz)
- ¼ cup shredded fresh basil leaves

1 Spray 4½- to 5-quart slow cooker with cooking spray. Mix mushrooms, onions, melted butter, soy sauce, salt and pepper in slow cooker. Pour vegetable broth over vegetable mixture.

2 Cover; cook on Low heat setting 7 to 8 hours or until vegetables are very tender and browned.

3 Stir in tortellini and cream cheese. Cover; cook on Low heat setting 15 minutes. Cook and stir 14 to 16 minutes longer or until tortellini are tender. Stir in spinach. Let stand 5 minutes. Top with Parmesan cheese and basil.

1 Serving: Calories 430; Total Fat 29g (Saturated Fat 17g, Trans Fat 1g); Cholesterol 150mg; Sodium 1640mg; Total Carbohydrate 25g (Dietary Fiber 2g); Protein 15g **Exchanges:** 1 Starch, 2 Vegetable, 1 High-Fat Meat, 4 Fat **Carbohydrate Choices:** 1½

Genius Tip Save time by purchasing presliced mushrooms.

Genius Tip The sauce in this recipe will be thin after stirring in the spinach, but it will thicken after standing.

Instant Pot

Creamy Tuscan Chicken Pasta

Prep Time: 15 Minutes • Start to Finish: 45 Minutes • 6 servings (about 1½ cups each)

- 1 carton (32 oz) chicken broth
- ½ cup chopped sun-dried tomatoes in oil and herbs, drained
- 1 tablespoon Italian seasoning
- ½ teaspoon salt
- ¼ teaspoon crushed red pepper flakes
- 1 package (20 oz) boneless skinless chicken thighs, cut into 1-inch pieces
- 12 oz uncooked campanelle pasta (4 cups)
- 1 package (5 oz) fresh baby spinach leaves
- 1 package (8 oz) cream cheese, cut into cubes, softened
- 1 cup shredded Parmesan cheese (4 oz)

1 Spray 6-quart Instant Pot™ insert with cooking spray. Mix broth, tomatoes, Italian seasoning, salt and pepper flakes in insert. Stir in chicken and pasta.

2 Secure lid; set pressure valve to **SEALING**. Select **MANUAL/PRESSURE COOK**; cook on high pressure 7 minutes. Select **CANCEL**. Set pressure valve to **VENTING** to quick-release pressure.

3 Once pressure has released (about 5 minutes), immediately stir mixture 1 to 2 minutes or until pasta is completely separated. Pasta will appear to be stuck together but will separate while stirring. Stir in spinach, cream cheese and Parmesan cheese until cheeses melt. Let stand 5 minutes.

1 Serving: Calories 610; Total Fat 25g (Saturated Fat 12g, Trans Fat 0.5g); Cholesterol 140mg; Sodium 1240mg; Total Carbohydrate 56g (Dietary Fiber 4g); Protein 40g **Exchanges:** 2 Starch, 1½ Other Carbohydrate, 1 Vegetable, 4 Very Lean Meat, ½ High-Fat Meat, 3½ Fat **Carbohydrate Choices:** 4

Genius Tip Campanelle pasta is a ruffled, bell-shaped pasta. It is excellent with thick, creamy sauces.

Ranch Chicken Pasta

Prep Time: 10 Minutes • Start to Finish: 45 Minutes • 6 servings (1⅔ cups each)

1 can (18 oz) creamy mushroom soup

2¼ cups chicken broth (from 32-oz carton)

1 can (14.5 oz) fire-roasted crushed tomatoes

1 can (4.5 oz) chopped green chiles

1 package (0.85 oz) chicken taco seasoning mix

1 package (20 oz) boneless skinless chicken thighs, cut into 1-inch pieces

12 oz uncooked penne pasta (3½ cups)

2 cups shredded sharp Cheddar cheese (8 oz)

Chopped fresh cilantro, crushed tortilla chips and sour cream, if desired

1 Spray 6-quart Instant Pot™ insert with cooking spray. Mix soup, broth, tomatoes, chiles and taco seasoning mix in insert. Stir in chicken and pasta.

2 Secure lid; set pressure valve to **SEALING**. Select **MANUAL/PRESSURE COOK**; cook on high pressure 7 minutes. Select **CANCEL**. Set pressure valve to **VENTING** to quick-release pressure.

3 Once pressure has released (about 5 minutes), immediately stir mixture 1 to 2 minutes or until pasta is completely separated. Pasta will appear to be stuck together but will separate while stirring. Stir in cheese. Let stand 5 minutes. Top with remaining ingredients.

1 Serving: Calories 600; Total Fat 22g (Saturated Fat 9g, Trans Fat 0g); Cholesterol 130mg; Sodium 1380mg; Total Carbohydrate 62g (Dietary Fiber 3g); Protein 39g **Exchanges:** 2½ Starch, 1½ Other Carbohydrate, 3½ Very Lean Meat, 1 High-Fat Meat, 2 Fat **Carbohydrate Choices:** 4

Customize It If you like spicy food, serve this hearty dish with Mexican hot sauce or chopped pickled jalapeños.

Genius Tip Chicken thighs stay moist and tender in the Instant Pot™, making them a better choice than chicken breasts for this recipe.

5-Ingredient Cheesy Chicken, Broccoli and Rice

Prep Time: 10 Minutes • Start to Finish: 35 Minutes • 4 servings

1½ cups chicken broth (from 32-oz carton)

1 cup uncooked long-grain white rice

½ teaspoon salt

¼ teaspoon pepper

1 package (20 oz) boneless skinless chicken thighs, cut into 1-inch pieces

1 package (10 oz) fresh broccoli florets (about 4 cups)

1 cup shredded sharp Cheddar cheese (4 oz)

1 Spray 6-quart Instant Pot™ insert with cooking spray. Mix broth, rice, salt and pepper in insert. Stir in chicken and broccoli.

2 Secure lid; set pressure valve to **SEALING**. Select **MANUAL/PRESSURE COOK**; cook on high pressure 10 minutes. Select **CANCEL**. Set pressure valve to **VENTING** to quick-release pressure.

3 Once pressure has released (about 5 minutes), stir in cheese. Broccoli may start to fall apart while stirring.

1 Serving: Calories 500; Total Fat 17g (Saturated Fat 7g, Trans Fat 0g); Cholesterol 165mg; Sodium 920mg; Total Carbohydrate 46g (Dietary Fiber 2g); Protein 42g **Exchanges:** 2½ Starch, 1 Vegetable, 4 Very Lean Meat, ½ High-Fat Meat, 2 Fat **Carbohydrate Choices:** 3

Genius Tip While precut bagged broccoli florets make an easy shortcut, you can also cut your own. One large head of broccoli will provide plenty of florets for this recipe.

Genius Tip We used chicken thighs instead of chicken breasts in this recipe so that the chicken is still tender by the time the rice is cooked through.

"Roast" Herbed Chicken

I cup unsalted chicken broth (from 32-oz carton)

I small onion, peeled, quartered

I whole chicken (3 to 4 lb), giblets removed

4 tablespoons butter, melted

2 teaspoons chopped fresh thyme leaves

I teaspoon salt

I teaspoon paprika

½ teaspoon pepper

3 tablespoons cornstarch

3 tablespoons cold water

1 Spray 6-quart Instant Pot™ with cooking spray. Add broth to insert; place rack in bottom of insert. Place onion inside chicken cavity; tie legs with cooking twine. Pat chicken dry with paper towels. In small bowl, mix melted butter, thyme, salt, paprika and pepper; brush on chicken. Place chicken, breast side up, on rack.

2 Secure lid; set pressure valve to **SEALING**. Select **MANUAL/PRESSURE COOK**; cook on high pressure 27 minutes. Select **CANCEL**. Keep pressure valve in **SEALING** position to release pressure naturally. Internal temperature in thigh should be at least 165°F using instant-read thermometer. If chicken is not done, select **MANUAL/PRESSURE COOK** and cook on high pressure 2 to 5 minutes longer. Select **CANCEL**. Keep pressure valve in **SEALING** position to release pressure naturally until all pressure is released.

3 When cool enough to handle, carefully transfer chicken to cutting board; remove rack.

4 Select **SAUTÉ**; adjust to normal. Heat liquid to simmering. In small bowl, beat cornstarch and cold water; stir into liquid, and cook I to 2 minutes or until thickened. Select **CANCEL**.

5 Carve chicken; serve with gravy.

I Serving: Calories 480; Total Fat 32g (Saturated Fat 13g, Trans Fat 1g); Cholesterol 160mg; Sodium 830mg; Total Carbohydrate 8g (Dietary Fiber 0g); Protein 41g **Exchanges:** ½ Other Carbohydrate, 6 Lean Meat, 3 Fat **Carbohydrate Choices:** ½

Customize It If crispy skin is desired, place carved chicken, skin side up, on foil-lined baking pan, and broil 4 inches from broiler element 3 to 5 minutes or until skin is crisp and browned.

Genius Tip Larger chickens may require a slightly longer cook time.

Chicken Pot Pie

Prep Time: 30 Minutes • **Start to Finish: 45 Minutes** • **4 servings**

1 lb boneless skinless chicken breasts, cut into 1-inch pieces

1 teaspoon salt

¾ teaspoon poultry seasoning

2 tablespoons butter

1½ cups chicken broth (from 32-oz carton)

2 cups diced peeled russet potatoes

1 package (12 oz) frozen mixed vegetables

3 tablespoons cornstarch

3 tablespoons water

1 refrigerated pie crust, softened as directed on box

1 Heat oven to 450°F. Line large cookie sheet with cooking parchment paper. Spray 6-quart Instant Pot™ insert with cooking spray. In medium bowl, toss chicken pieces with salt and poultry seasoning. Select **SAUTÉ**; adjust to normal. Melt butter in insert. Add chicken. Cook 3 to 4 minutes without moving, until browned on first side; then turn and cook 2 to 4 minutes or until chicken is browned on second side. Select **CANCEL**.

2 Stir in broth, potatoes and mixed vegetables. Secure lid; set pressure valve to **SEALING**. Select **MANUAL/PRESSURE COOK**; cook on high pressure 2 minutes. Select **CANCEL**. Set pressure valve to **VENTING** to quick-release pressure.

3 In small bowl, beat cornstarch and water with whisk. Once pressure has released, select **SAUTÉ**, and adjust to normal; heat liquid to simmering. Beat in cornstarch mixture; cook 30 to 60 seconds, beating frequently with whisk, until thickened. Select **CANCEL**.

4 Meanwhile, unroll crust on work surface. With 2½-inch round cutter, cut 16 rounds from crust, rerolling once; discard scraps. Place pie crust rounds on cookie sheet. Bake 7 to 9 minutes or until golden brown and crisp. Immediately remove from cookie sheet to cooling rack.

5 Spoon chicken mixture into bowls. Top with pie crust rounds.

1 Serving: Calories 510; Total Fat 22g (Saturated Fat 10g, Trans Fat 0g); Cholesterol 95mg; Sodium 1290mg; Total Carbohydrate 48g (Dietary Fiber 3g); Protein 30g **Exchanges:** 2 Starch, ½ Other Carbohydrate, 1½ Vegetable, 3 Very Lean Meat, 4 Fat **Carbohydrate Choices:** 3

Make It a Meal
Serve the pot pie with sliced fresh tomatoes and cucumbers drizzled with Italian dressing.

Genius Tip
For best browning, pat chicken pieces dry before tossing with salt and poultry seasoning.

Sweet-and-Sour Pineapple Beef Brisket

Prep Time: 40 Minutes • Start to Finish: 1 Hour 20 Minutes • 8 servings

2 tablespoons vegetable oil

1 (2¼ lb) fresh beef brisket (not corned beef), cut into thirds

1 teaspoon garlic-pepper blend

1 teaspoon salt

1 can (20 oz) pineapple chunks in juice, drained, ½ cup juice reserved

3 tablespoons apple cider vinegar

2 tablespoons packed brown sugar

3 cloves garlic, finely chopped

1½ lb red fingerling potatoes

1 medium onion, cut into wedges

3 tablespoons cornstarch

¼ teaspoon crushed red pepper flakes

1 small head cabbage, cut into 8 wedges (about 1½ lb)

1 large red bell pepper, cut into 1-inch pieces

1 On 6-quart Instant Pot™, select **SAUTÉ**; adjust to normal. Heat oil in insert. Sprinkle brisket pieces with garlic-pepper blend and ½ teaspoon of the salt. Cook 1 to 2 pieces of the brisket at a time in insert. Cook 4 to 6 minutes, turning once, until browned; remove to plate. Select **CANCEL**.

2 Meanwhile, in medium bowl, mix ¼ cup of the pineapple juice, the vinegar, brown sugar and garlic.

3 Pour over brisket in insert. Add potatoes and onion. Secure lid; set pressure valve to **SEALING**. Select **MANUAL/PRESSURE COOK**; cook on high pressure 20 minutes. Select **CANCEL**. Keep pressure valve in **SEALING** position to release pressure naturally, about 30 minutes. Set pressure valve to **VENTING**.

4 Meanwhile, in small bowl, mix the remaining ¼ cup pineapple juice, the cornstarch, remaining ½ teaspoon salt and red pepper flakes.

5 Open lid; transfer the potatoes and onion to large serving platter. Transfer brisket to cutting board; cover with foil. Select **SAUTÉ**. Add cabbage, bell pepper and pineapple chunks; cook 6 to 8 minutes or until cabbage is tender. Using slotted spoon, remove vegetables and pineapple to serving platter. Cut beef across grain into thin slices; transfer to serving platter.

6 Add pineapple juice mixture to pot; cook and stir 1 to 2 minutes or until sauce is thickened. Brush 1 tablespoon sauce over beef; serve remaining sauce with vegetables and beef.

1 Serving: Calories 390; Total Fat 12g (Saturated Fat 3.5g, Trans Fat 0g); Cholesterol 80mg; Sodium 410mg; Total Carbohydrate 39g (Dietary Fiber 5g); Protein 31g **Exchanges:** 1½ Starch, ½ Fruit, 2½ Vegetable, 3 Lean Meat, ½ Fat **Carbohydrate Choices:** 2½

Customize It Fingerling potatoes are small, narrow, finger-shaped potatoes. They come in a variety of colors, so choose the color you prefer. To add a splash of color, try red cabbage instead of the green cabbage.

Genius Tip This recipe calls for fresh beef brisket, not to be confused with corned beef, which uses the same cut of meat but is brined. This inexpensive, less-tender cut of meat requires a long, slow cook time to create moist, tender beef. The Instant Pot™ cuts the cooking time drastically, from 6 to 8 hours in a slow cooker to just under an hour!

Classic Beef Stew

Prep Time: 45 Minutes • **Start to Finish: 1 Hour 50 Minutes** • **8 servings**

2 lb beef stew meat

2 teaspoons salt

1 teaspoon pepper

2 tablespoons butter

1 tablespoon tomato paste

2 cups chopped onions

2 cups 1-inch diced peeled carrots

2 cups 1-inch diced peeled russet potatoes

1 cup beef broth (from 32-oz carton)

2 tablespoons cornstarch

2 tablespoons water

1 In large bowl, mix beef with salt and pepper. Spray 6-quart Instant Pot™ insert with cooking spray. Select **SAUTÉ**; adjust to normal. Melt butter in insert. Add beef in 2 batches; cook 2 to 4 minutes on first side until browned. Turn beef; cook 2 to 4 minutes on second side or until browned. Select **CANCEL**. Return beef to insert.

2 Stir in tomato paste, onions, carrots and potatoes. Stir in broth.

3 Secure lid; set pressure valve to **SEALING**. Select **MANUAL/PRESSURE COOK**; cook on high pressure 45 minutes. Select **CANCEL**. Set pressure valve to **VENTING** to quick-release pressure.

4 In small bowl, beat cornstarch and water with whisk. Once pressure has released (about 5 minutes), select **SAUTÉ**; adjust to normal. Heat liquid to boiling. Gently stir in cornstarch mixture; cook 30 to 60 seconds, stirring frequently, until thickened. Select **CANCEL**.

1 Serving: Calories 290; Total Fat 15g (Saturated Fat 7g, Trans Fat 0.5g); Cholesterol 70mg; Sodium 790mg; Total Carbohydrate 16g (Dietary Fiber 2g); Protein 22g **Exchanges:** 1 Other Carbohydrate, ½ Vegetable, 3 Medium-Fat Meat **Carbohydrate Choices:** 1

Genius Tip Instead of 2 pounds of stew meat, you can purchase a 2½- to 3-pound beef chuck roast, and cut it yourself. Trim off the fat, and cut into 2-inch pieces. You should end up with about 2 pounds of meat.

Genius Tip Top with chopped fresh parsley for a pretty, fresh garnish.

Beef and Black Bean Chili

Prep Time: 15 Minutes • Start to Finish: 55 Minutes • 6 servings

1 tablespoon vegetable oil

1 lb extra-lean (at least 90%) ground beef

2 cups chopped onions

1 tablespoon chili powder

½ teaspoon salt

1 can (28 oz) fire-roasted crushed tomatoes, undrained

1 can (15 oz) black beans, drained, rinsed

1 can (4.5 oz) chopped green chiles

½ cup water

1 On 6-quart Instant Pot™, select **SAUTÉ**; adjust to normal. Heat oil in insert. Add beef, onions, chili powder and salt. Cook 8 to 10 minutes, stirring occasionally, until thoroughly cooked. Select **CANCEL**.

2 Stir in tomatoes, beans, chiles and water.

3 Secure lid; set pressure valve to **SEALING**. Select **MANUAL/PRESSURE COOK**; cook on high pressure 5 minutes. Select **CANCEL**. Keep pressure valve in **SEALING** position to release pressure naturally until all pressure has been released (about 30 minutes).

1 Serving: Calories 290; Total Fat 11g (Saturated Fat 3.5g, Trans Fat 0g); Cholesterol 45mg; Sodium 760mg; Total Carbohydrate 30g (Dietary Fiber 7g); Protein 19g **Exchanges:** ½ Starch, 1½ Other Carbohydrate, 2½ Very Lean Meat, 2 Fat **Carbohydrate Choices:** 2

Customize It Top with shredded Colby–Monterey Jack cheese, sour cream, chopped fresh cilantro or green onions.

Genius Tip When releasing pressure naturally, it's always a good idea to set the pressure valve to **VENTING** after the float valve drops down, just to be sure all of the pressure has been released.

Beef Barbacoa

2   tablespoons vegetable oil

2   lb beef stew meat

1   cup beef broth
    (from 32-oz carton)

2   tablespoons finely
    chopped chipotle chiles
    in adobo sauce

3   cloves garlic, finely
    chopped

1   package (1 oz) original
    taco seasoning mix

1   teaspoon ground cumin

1   teaspoon ground
    coriander

¼   teaspoon salt

2   cups chopped red onions

1   Spray 6-quart Instant Pot™ insert with cooking spray. Select **SAUTÉ**; adjust to normal. Heat oil in insert. Add beef in 2 batches; cook 2 to 4 minutes on first side until browned. Turn; cook 2 to 4 minutes on second side until browned. Select **CANCEL**. Return beef to insert.

2   Add broth, chiles in adobo sauce, garlic, taco seasoning mix, cumin, coriander and salt to beef in insert. Stir in onions.

3   Secure lid; set pressure valve to **SEALING**. Select **MANUAL/PRESSURE COOK**; cook on high pressure 45 minutes. Select **CANCEL**. Set pressure valve to **VENTING** to quick-release pressure.

4   Once all pressure has been released (about 5 minutes), shred beef, using 2 forks; toss with ½ cup of the cooking liquid. Discard any remaining cooking liquid.

1 Serving: Calories 310; Total Fat 18g (Saturated Fat 7g, Trans Fat 0.5g); Cholesterol 80mg; Sodium 340mg; Total Carbohydrate 8g (Dietary Fiber 1g); Protein 28g **Exchanges:** ½ Other Carbohydrate, ½ Vegetable, 4 Lean Meat, 1 Fat **Carbohydrate Choices:** ½

Genius Tip You can easily substitute a 2½- to 3-lb boneless beef chuck roast for the beef stew meat. Cut into 1½- to 2-inch cubes, and trim off any large pieces of fat before browning.

Spaghetti Bolognese

Prep Time: 25 Minutes • Start to Finish: 50 Minutes • 6 servings

1 tablespoon olive oil

1 lb extra-lean (at least 90%) ground beef

2 cups chopped onions

½ teaspoon salt

1 cup chopped celery

1 cup chopped peeled carrots

2 cups beef broth (from 32-oz carton)

12 oz uncooked spaghetti, broken in half

1 can (28 oz) fire-roasted crushed tomatoes, undrained

1 On 6-quart Instant Pot™, select **SAUTÉ**; adjust to normal. Heat oil in insert. Add beef, onions and salt; cook 8 to 10 minutes, stirring occasionally, until thoroughly cooked. Stir in celery and carrots. Select **CANCEL**.

2 Stir broth into beef mixture. Add spaghetti evenly over beef mixture. Spread tomatoes evenly over spaghetti.

3 Secure lid; set pressure valve to **SEALING**. Select **MANUAL/PRESSURE COOK**; cook on high pressure 7 minutes. Select **CANCEL**. Set pressure valve to **VENTING** to quick-release pressure.

4 Once all pressure has been released (about 5 minutes), using tongs, immediately lift and stir mixture 1 to 2 minutes or until pasta is completely separated. Spaghetti will appear to be stuck together but will separate while stirring.

1 Serving: Calories 460; Total Fat 10g (Saturated Fat 3g, Trans Fat 0g); Cholesterol 50mg; Sodium 760mg; Total Carbohydrate 68g (Dietary Fiber 5g); Protein 26g **Exchanges:** 3 Starch, 1½ Other Carbohydrate, ½ Vegetable, 2 Very Lean Meat, 1½ Fat **Carbohydrate Choices:** 4½

Customize It For a pretty (and tasty) finishing touch, sprinkle with shredded Parmesan cheese and thinly sliced fresh basil leaves.

Genius Tip Try to evenly cover the pasta with the tomatoes. This helps the pasta cook evenly under pressure.

Spaghetti with Meatballs

Prep Time: 25 Minutes • **Start to Finish: 50 Minutes** • **6 servings (1⅓ cups each)**

1 lb extra-lean (at least 90%) ground beef

½ cup Italian-style panko crispy bread crumbs

½ cup chopped onion

¼ cup milk

1 egg, slightly beaten

3 cloves garlic, finely chopped

2 teaspoons Worcestershire sauce

½ teaspoon salt

½ teaspoon pepper

1 tablespoon olive oil

1 jar (24.5 oz) tomato basil pasta sauce

2½ cups beef broth (from 32-oz carton)

12 oz uncooked spaghetti, broken in half

Shredded Parmesan cheese, if desired

Shredded fresh basil leaves, if desired

1 In large bowl, mix beef, bread crumbs, onion, milk, egg, garlic, Worcestershire sauce, salt and pepper. Shape mixture into 12 (2-inch) meatballs.

2 On 6-quart Instant Pot™, select **SAUTÉ**; adjust to normal. Heat oil in insert. Add meatballs; cook 4 to 5 minutes without moving, until meatballs release easily from bottom of insert. Turn; cook 2 to 3 minutes or until browned on second side. Turn one more time; cook 2 to 3 minutes on third side, until browned. Select **CANCEL**. Using tongs, transfer meatballs to plate.

3 Stir pasta sauce and broth into meatball drippings in insert. Stir mixture to loosen browned bits from bottom of insert. Stir in spaghetti; coat in sauce mixture. Place meatballs evenly over spaghetti mixture.

4 Secure lid; set pressure valve to **SEALING**. Select **MANUAL/PRESSURE COOK**; cook on high pressure 8 minutes. Select **CANCEL**. Set pressure valve to **VENTING** to quick-release pressure.

5 Once all pressure has been released (about 5 minutes), gently stir mixture 30 to 60 seconds or until spaghetti is completely separated. Spaghetti will appear to be stuck together but will separate while stirring. Let stand 5 minutes. Top with Parmesan and basil.

1 Serving: Calories 530; Total Fat 16g (Saturated Fat 4g, Trans Fat 0g); Cholesterol 80mg; Sodium 1280mg; Total Carbohydrate 68g (Dietary Fiber 5g); Protein 28g **Exchanges:** 2½ Starch, 2 Other Carbohydrate, ½ Vegetable, 2½ Very Lean Meat, 2½ Fat **Carbohydrate Choices:** 4½

Genius Tip Be careful not to turn meatballs before they are fully browned. This can cause the tender meatballs to tear.

Genius Tip It's important to use 90% extra-lean ground beef for this recipe to prevent sauce from being too fatty.

Pho-Style Pot Roast Dinner

Prep Time: 25 Minutes • **Start to Finish: 1 Hour 20 Minutes** • **6 servings**

1 tablespoon vegetable oil

1 boneless beef chuck roast (2 lb), cut into 4 pieces

½ teaspoon salt

¼ teaspoon pepper

1½ cups beef broth (from 32-oz carton)

¾ cup water

¼ cup rice wine vinegar

3 tablespoons fish sauce (from 6.76-oz bottle)

1 tablespoon grated fresh gingerroot

2 cloves garlic, finely chopped

1½ teaspoons five-spice powder

3 pieces (3 inches each) lemon grass stalk, crushed slightly with meat mallet to break outer layers

2 large sweet potatoes (1½ lb), peeled, cut into 1-inch pieces (4 cups)

7 oz uncooked rice noodles (from 14-oz package)

1 small red bell pepper, cut into very thin strips or fresh red Thai peppers, sliced

6 lime slices, cut in half

6 sprigs fresh Thai basil, if desired

1 Spray 6-quart Instant Pot™ with cooking spray. Select **SAUTÉ**; adjust to normal. Heat oil in insert. Sprinkle beef pieces with salt and pepper. Cook half of the beef 2 to 3 minutes on first side until browned; turn. Cook 2 to 3 minutes on second side or until browned; transfer to plate. Repeat with remaining beef pieces. Select **CANCEL**. Place all beef pieces in insert.

2 Mix broth, water, vinegar, fish sauce, gingerroot, garlic, five-spice powder and lemon grass in insert. Place sweet potatoes on top of beef.

3 Secure lid; set pressure valve to **SEALING**. Select **MANUAL/PRESSURE COOK**; cook on high pressure 45 minutes. Select **CANCEL**. Set pressure valve to **VENTING** to quick-release pressure. Once all pressure has been released, remove beef and sweet potatoes with slotted spoon; cover with foil to keep warm.

4 Select **SAUTÉ**. Heat liquid in insert to boiling. Stir noodles into liquid mixture. Select **CANCEL**. Cover; let stand 10 minutes or until noodles are soft yet firm.

5 To serve, place meat on cutting board. Break into bite-size pieces with 2 forks. Using tongs, place about ½ cup of the noodles into each individual serving bowl. Top each with beef pieces and sweet potatoes. Pour ⅓ cup broth over meat and potatoes. Top with red bell pepper strips and lime slices. Garnish with basil.

1 Serving: Calories 460; Total Fat 19g (Saturated Fat 7g, Trans Fat 0.5g); Cholesterol 80mg; Sodium 1240mg; Total Carbohydrate 40g (Dietary Fiber 3g); Protein 32g **Exchanges:** 1 Starch, 1½ Other Carbohydrate, ½ Vegetable, 4 Lean Meat, 1½ Fat **Carbohydrate Choices:** 2½

Genius Tip This creative recipe combines the trendy flavors and components of the Vietnamese soup, *pho,* with the melt-in-your-mouth tenderness of a traditional American pot roast. It's worth cutting the roast into 4 pieces before cooking it as this allows the meat to cook until very tender while everything else gets done.

Find It For a more robust flavor, add 2 star anise with the lemon grass. Star anise adds the sweet and spicy licorice-like flavor used in Vietnamese cuisine to flavor pho. It can be found either in the spice aisle, in the produce section or where other Asian ingredients are located.

Creole-Style Pork Chop Dinner

1 tablespoon vegetable oil

4 bone-in pork loin or rib chops, about ¾ inch thick (about 2 lb)

¼ teaspoon salt

¼ teaspoon pepper

2 medium green bell peppers, cut into 1½-inch strips (2 cups)

1 large onion, cut into 1½-inch strips (1 cup)

½ lb fully cooked kielbasa sausage, thinly sliced

2 cloves garlic, finely chopped

1⅓ cups chicken broth (from 32-oz carton)

1 can (14.5 oz) fire-roasted diced tomatoes, undrained

¾ cup uncooked long-grain white rice

1½ teaspoons Creole or Cajun seasoning

1 On 6-quart Instant Pot™, select **SAUTÉ**; adjust to normal. Heat oil in insert. Sprinkle pork chops with salt and pepper. Add 2 pork chops; cook about 2 minutes on each side just until brown. Remove from insert. Repeat with remaining 2 pork chops, removing from insert after browning.

2 Add bell peppers, onion, sausage and garlic to insert; cook 4 to 5 minutes, stirring occasionally to remove any browned bits from bottom of insert, until onions and peppers are crisp-tender. Select **CANCEL**.

3 Stir in broth, tomatoes, rice and Creole seasoning. Submerge pork chops evenly into rice mixture by pushing them down into it and spooning it over the tops of the pork chops.

4 Secure lid; set pressure valve to **SEALING**. Select **MANUAL/PRESSURE COOK**; cook on high pressure 8 minutes. Select **CANCEL**. Set pressure valve to **VENTING** to quick-release pressure. Once all pressure has been removed (about 5 minutes), remove pork chops from pot to serving platter; cover with foil. Stir rice mixture; let stand 5 minutes until most of the liquid is absorbed.

1 Serving: Calories 650; Total Fat 32g (Saturated Fat 11g, Trans Fat 0.5g); Cholesterol 135mg; Sodium 1420mg; Total Carbohydrate 44g (Dietary Fiber 3g); Protein 46g **Exchanges:** 1 Starch, 2 Other Carbohydrate, ½ Vegetable, 4 Very Lean Meat, 2 High-Fat Meat, 2½ Fat **Carbohydrate Choices:** 3

Customize It
For an added spicy kick, try out this recipe using smoked andouille or chorizo sausage.

Genius Tip
Completely covering the pork chops with the rice mixture makes them juicy and flavorful. Submerging the pork chops creates juices to hydrate the rice and also liquid that the Instant Pot™ needs to get to high pressure.

5-Ingredient Barbecue Pork Ribs

Prep Time: 15 Minutes • Start to Finish: 1 Hour 10 Minutes • 4 servings

1 cup chicken broth (from 32-oz carton)

1 tablespoon barbecue seasoning

1 tablespoon Worcestershire sauce

3 lb pork baby back ribs, cut into 4 (3- to 4-rib) sections

½ cup sweet & spicy barbecue sauce

1 Spray 6-quart Instant Pot™ insert with cooking spray. Mix broth, seasoning and Worcestershire sauce in insert. Add ribs; turn to coat. Stand ribs up against sides of insert.

2 Secure lid; set pressure valve to **SEALING**. Select **MANUAL/PRESSURE COOK**; cook on high pressure 15 minutes. Select **CANCEL**. Keep pressure valve in **SEALING** position to release pressure naturally (about 30 minutes). Transfer ribs to cutting board; cool slightly. Discard cooking liquid. When cool enough to handle, cut sections into individual ribs. Brush ribs with barbecue sauce on all sides.

1 Serving: Calories 460; Total Fat 30g (Saturated Fat 11g, Trans Fat 0g); Cholesterol 135mg; Sodium 1000mg; Total Carbohydrate 11g (Dietary Fiber 1g); Protein 37g **Exchanges:** ½ Other Carbohydrate, 5½ Medium-Fat Meat, ½ Fat **Carbohydrate Choices:** 1

Genius Tip Give the ribs nicely browned edges, as if they were baked in the oven, by placing the sauced, cooked ribs on an 18×13-inch rimmed sheet pan lined with foil and sprayed with cooking spray. Broil ribs 4 inches from heat or until barbecue sauce is sticky and blackened in spots.

Genius Tip Don't substitute larger ribs for the baby back ribs. This recipe was designed for the smaller racks, and larger ribs will not get tender in the same amount of time.

5-Ingredient Pork Shoulder

Prep Time: 30 Minutes • **Start to Finish: 2 Hours 35 Minutes** • **12 servings**

2 tablespoons butter

1 boneless pork shoulder roast (3 to 4 lb), trimmed of excess fat, cut in 3 pieces

1 cup chicken broth (from 32-oz carton)

2 tablespoons packed brown sugar

2 tablespoons soy sauce

10 cloves garlic, finely chopped

1 teaspoon salt

1 On 6-quart Instant Pot™, select **SAUTÉ**; adjust to normal. Melt butter in insert. Add pork; cook 2 to 4 minutes on all sides or until browned. Select **CANCEL**.

2 In small bowl, mix broth, brown sugar, soy sauce, garlic and salt. Pour over pork in insert.

3 Secure lid; set pressure valve to **SEALING**. Select **MANUAL/PRESSURE COOK**; cook on high pressure 90 minutes. Select **CANCEL**. Keep pressure valve in **SEALING** position to release pressure naturally (about 30 minutes).

4 When cool enough to handle, shred pork, using 2 forks; toss with 1 cup of the cooking liquid. Discard remaining cooking liquid.

1 Serving: Calories 230, Total Fat 15g (Saturated Fat 6g, Trans Fat 0g), Cholesterol 75mg; Sodium 190mg; Total Carbohydrate 0g (Dietary Fiber 0g); Protein 23g **Exchanges:** 3½ Very Lean Meat, 2½ Fat **Carbohydrate Choices:** 0

Make It a Meal
This pulled pork works well stuffed into tacos or pitas, served over rice or mashed potatoes, or spooned into buns.

Genius Tip
Cutting the pork in several large pieces allows the meat to cook quickly and evenly in the pressure cooker.

Genius Tip
When releasing pressure naturally, it's always a good idea to set the pressure valve to **VENTING** after the float valve drops down, just to be sure all of the pressure has been released.

Creamy Garlic Pork Chops

Prep Time: 10 Minutes • Start to Finish: 25 Minutes • 4 servings

1 cup chicken broth
(from 32-oz carton)

4 cloves garlic, finely
chopped

½ teaspoon salt

½ teaspoon pepper

4 bone-in pork loin chops
(1¾ lb)

2 tablespoons cornstarch

2 tablespoons water

4 oz cream cheese,
softened, cubed

1 Spray 6-quart Instant Pot™ insert with cooking spray. Add broth to insert. Stir in garlic, salt and pepper. Add pork chops to broth mixture in insert.

2 Secure lid; set pressure valve to **SEALING**. Select **MANUAL/PRESSURE COOK**; cook on high pressure 2 minutes. Select **CANCEL**. Set pressure valve to **VENTING** to quick-release pressure. Once all pressure has been released (about 5 minutes), internal temperature of pork should be at least 145°F using instant-read thermometer. If pork is not done, select **MANUAL/PRESSURE** and cook on high pressure 1 to 2 minutes longer. Select **CANCEL**. Set pressure valve to **VENTING** to quick-release pressure.

3 Once all pressure has been released (about 5 minutes), remove pork chops from pot; place on plate. Cover with foil to keep warm.

4 In small bowl, beat cornstarch and water with whisk. Select **SAUTÉ**, and adjust to normal; heat liquid to simmering. Beat in cornstarch mixture; cook 30 to 60 seconds, beating frequently with whisk, until thickened. Select **CANCEL**. Beat in cream cheese with whisk until smooth. Serve over pork chops.

1 Serving: Calories 340; Total Fat 21g (Saturated Fat 10g, Trans Fat 0g); Cholesterol 120mg; Sodium 640mg; Total Carbohydrate 7g (Dietary Fiber 0g); Protein 33g **Exchanges:** ½ Low-Fat Milk, 4 Very Lean Meat, 3½ Fat **Carbohydrate Choices:** ½

Customize It For a pretty pop of green on top, sprinkle with chopped fresh parsley leaves.

Genius Tip If juices collect on the plate while pork chops rest, pour off the accumulated liquid, and discard before topping with the creamy garlic sauce.

Genius Tip Be sure to purchase thin bone-in pork chops. Thicker-cut chops won't get done in this short cook time.

Cuban Pork Tenderloin with Rice and Beans

Prep Time: 20 Minutes • Start to Finish: 40 Minutes • 4 servings (about 1½ cups each)

2 tablespoons vegetable oil

1 pork tenderloin (1¼ lb), trimmed, cut into 1-inch pieces

1¼ cups chicken broth (from 32-oz carton)

½ cup orange juice

1 package (1 oz) taco seasoning mix

5 cloves garlic, finely chopped

1 teaspoon ground cumin

1 can (15 oz) black beans, drained, rinsed

1 cup uncooked regular long-grain white rice

1 tablespoon fresh lime juice

2 tablespoons chopped fresh cilantro

Chunky-style salsa, if desired

1 On 6-quart Instant Pot™, select **SAUTÉ**; adjust to normal. Heat oil in insert. Add pork; cook 4 to 6 minutes or until pork releases easily from bottom of insert. Stir. Select **CANCEL**.

2 Stir in broth, orange juice, taco seasoning mix, garlic and cumin. Stir in beans and rice.

3 Secure lid; set pressure valve to **SEALING**. Select **MANUAL/PRESSURE COOK**; cook on high pressure 12 minutes. Select **CANCEL**. Set pressure valve to **VENTING** to quick-release pressure.

4 Once all pressure has been released (about 5 minutes) stir in lime juice. Top with cilantro. Serve with salsa.

1 Serving: Calories 530; Total Fat 14g (Saturated Fat 3g, Trans Fat 0g); Cholesterol 85mg; Sodium 1050mg; Total Carbohydrate 62g (Dietary Fiber 4g); Protein 40g **Exchanges:** 3 Starch, 1 Other Carbohydrate, 4½ Very Lean Meat, 2 Fat **Carbohydrate Choices:** 4

Genius Tip Don't skip the step of trimming the pork tenderloin. That membrane doesn't cook away, and it prevents flavors and seasonings from getting to the meat. To remove silverskin, run a knife underneath the shiny membrane while removing as little meat as possible.

Split Pea Soup with Ham

Prep Time: 25 Minutes • **Start to Finish: 1 Hour 55 Minutes** • **8 servings (1⅓ cups each)**

2 tablespoons butter

2 cups chopped onions

¼ teaspoon salt

¼ teaspoon pepper

3 cups diced cooked ham

1½ cups chopped carrots

½ cup chopped celery

4 cloves garlic, finely chopped

1 carton (32 oz) reduced-sodium chicken broth

2 cups water

2¼ cups dried split peas (1 lb), sorted, rinsed

1 On 6-quart Instant Pot™, select **SAUTÉ**; adjust to normal. Melt butter in insert. Add onions, salt and pepper; cook 6 to 8 minutes, stirring frequently, until softened. Select **CANCEL**.

2 Stir in ham, carrots, celery and garlic. Stir in broth and water; stir in peas.

3 Secure lid; set pressure valve to **SEALING**. Select **MANUAL/PRESSURE COOK**; cook on high pressure 15 minutes. Select **CANCEL**. Keep pressure valve in **SEALING** position to release pressure naturally (about 30 minutes). Stir; let stand 10 minutes.

1 Serving: Calories 300; Total Fat 6g (Saturated Fat 3g, Trans Fat 0g); Cholesterol 35mg; Sodium 990mg; Total Carbohydrate 37g (Dietary Fiber 16g); Protein 23g **Exchanges:** 2 Starch, 1 Vegetable, 2 Very Lean Meat, 1 Fat **Carbohydrate Choices:** 2½

Genius Tip After cooking thick soups and stews, always be sure to inspect the anti-block shield and exhaust valve in the lid of the Instant Pot™ to be sure they aren't blocked with food.

Tuna Noodle Casserole

Prep Time: 15 Minutes • **Start to Finish: 50 Minutes** • **5 servings (1⅓ cups each)**

2 tablespoons butter

1 medium onion, chopped (½ cup)

½ cup chopped red bell pepper

2 cloves garlic, finely chopped

2 teaspoons chopped fresh thyme leaves or ¾ teaspoon dried thyme leaves

2 tablespoons all-purpose flour

½ teaspoon salt

½ teaspoon pepper

1 carton (32 oz) vegetable or chicken broth

3 cups uncooked fusilli pasta

2 cans (5 oz each) tuna in water, drained

1 package (10 oz) frozen sugar snap peas

2 cups shredded Monterey Jack cheese (8 oz)

½ cup half-and-half

½ cup crushed corn chips

1 On 6-quart Instant Pot™, select **SAUTÉ**; adjust to high. Melt butter in insert. Stir onion, bell pepper, garlic and thyme into butter; cook, stirring occasionally until vegetables are tender. Stir in flour, salt and pepper until well mixed. Stir in broth and pasta.

2 Secure lid; set pressure valve to **SEALING**. Select **MANUAL/PRESSURE COOK**; cook on high pressure 12 minutes. Select **CANCEL**. Set pressure valve to **VENTING** to quick-release pressure.

3 Once all pressure has been released (about 5 minutes), stir in tuna, sugar snap peas, cheese and half-and-half. Select **SAUTÉ**; adjust to normal. Cook, stirring frequently, 2 to 4 minutes or until thoroughly heated and peas are crisp-tender. Select **CANCEL**. Sprinkle with corn chips.

1 Serving: Calories 720; Total Fat 26g (Saturated Fat 14g, Trans Fat 0.5g); Cholesterol 80mg; Sodium 1270mg; Total Carbohydrate 83g (Dietary Fiber 6g); Protein 37g **Exchanges:** 4½ Starch, ½ Other Carbohydrate, 1 Vegetable, 2 Lean Meat, 1 High-Fat Meat, 2 Fat **Carbohydrate Choices:** 5½

Genius Tip Fusilli is a spiral pasta, which works well with cream sauces because the twists hold all the delicious, flavorful sauce. Penne and rotini pasta are good substitutions for the fusilli.

Customize It What do you have on hand that's crunchy? Substitute any of these crunchy pantry staples for the corn chips: tortilla or potato chips, cheesy crackers or croutons.

Cheesy Enchilada Rice and Beans

Prep Time: 10 Minutes • Start to Finish: 35 Minutes • 4 servings (1½ cups each)

1 tablespoon vegetable oil

2 medium bell peppers, coarsely chopped (2 cups)

1 large onion, coarsely chopped (1 cup)

3 cloves garlic, finely chopped

1½ cups water

1 cup uncooked regular brown rice

1 can (10 oz) enchilada sauce

½ teaspoon salt

1 cup shredded Cheddar cheese (4 oz)

1 tablespoon chopped fresh cilantro

1 can (15 oz) black beans, drained, rinsed

½ cup corn chips

Sour cream, if desired

Chopped fresh cilantro, if desired

1 On 6-quart Instant Pot™, select **SAUTÉ**; adjust to normal. Heat oil in insert. Add bell peppers, onion and garlic; cook 2 to 3 minutes or until vegetables are tender. Stir. Select **CANCEL**.

2 Stir in water, rice, enchilada sauce and salt. Secure lid; set pressure valve to **SEALING**. Select **MANUAL/PRESSURE COOK**; cook on high pressure 22 minutes. Select **CANCEL**. Set pressure valve to **VENTING** to quick-release pressure.

3 Once the pressure has been released (about 5 minutes), stir in cheese, cilantro and beans. Cook and stir until cheese is melted and mixture is heated through. Top with corn chips, sour cream and cilantro.

1 Serving: Calories 580; Total Fat 18g (Saturated Fat 7g, Trans Fat 0g); Cholesterol 30mg; Sodium 1320mg; Total Carbohydrate 84g (Dietary Fiber 16g); Protein 21g **Exchanges:** 1 Starch, 4½ Other Carbohydrate, ⅓ Vegetable, 2 Very Lean Meat, ½ High-Fat Meat, 2½ Fat **Carbohydrate Choices:** 5½

Customize It This rice and bean one-dish meal can be used as a burrito filling, spooned on top of tortilla chips and shredded lettuce for a salad or served as a side dish (about 12 servings as a side dish) with tacos or fajitas. If you like a little more kick, add 1 teaspoon chili powder with the salt.

Genius Tip Be sure you are using regular, not instant, brown rice in this recipe. Brown rice has a nutty, chewy flavor and is nutrient and fiber dense.

Other Pans

Chicken Tamale Pie

Prep Time: 10 Minutes • Start to Finish: 40 Minutes • 6 servings

1 package (9 oz) frozen diced cooked chicken, thawed

1 can (4.5 oz) chopped green chiles, drained

2 teaspoons taco seasoning mix

1 cup shredded Mexican cheese blend (4 oz)

½ cup Original Bisquick® mix

½ cup cornmeal

¾ cup milk

1 egg

1 can (11 oz) whole kernel corn with red and green peppers, drained

Chunky-style salsa, if desired

1 Heat oven to 400°F. In 9-inch glass pie plate, stir chicken, chiles and taco seasoning mix until combined. Sprinkle with cheese.

2 In medium bowl, stir Bisquick mix, cornmeal, milk, egg and corn with whisk or fork until blended. Pour over chicken.

3 Bake 25 to 30 minutes or until toothpick inserted in topping comes out clean. Serve with salsa.

1 Serving: Calories 290; Total Fat 10g (Saturated Fat 5g, Trans Fat 0g); Cholesterol 90mg; Sodium 340mg; Total Carbohydrate 28g (Dietary Fiber 1g); Protein 22g **Exchanges:** 1 Starch, ½ Other Carbohydrate, ½ Vegetable, 2 Very Lean Meat, ½ High-Fat Meat, 1 Fat **Carbohydrate Choices:** 2

Customize It For a spicier pie, add a chopped canned chipotle chile to the chicken mixture.

Customize It For a beef version of the recipe, substitute 1 pound ground beef for the chicken. Cook the beef over medium heat 5 to 7 minutes, stirring occasionally, until browned; drain.

Favorite Chicken Nuggets

Prep Time: 15 Minutes • Start to Finish: 35 Minutes • 4 servings

3 cups bite-size squares oven-toasted corn cereal

½ cup grated Parmesan cheese

½ teaspoon salt

½ teaspoon seasoned salt

¼ teaspoon paprika

⅛ teaspoon garlic powder

3 tablespoons butter, melted

1 tablespoon milk

1 lb boneless skinless chicken breasts, cut into 1-inch cubes

1 Heat oven to 400°F. Line cookie sheet with foil. Place cereal in resealable food-storage plastic bag or between sheets of waxed paper; crush with rolling pin or meat mallet.

2 In medium bowl, mix crushed cereal, cheese, salt, seasoned salt, paprika and garlic powder. In small bowl, stir together melted butter and milk. Dip chicken into butter mixture, and then roll in cereal mixture to coat evenly. Place on cookie sheet.

3 Bake 17 to 20 minutes, turning once, until coating is light golden brown and chicken is no longer pink in center.

1 Serving: Calories 360; Total Fat 16g (Saturated Fat 9g, Trans Fat 0.5g); Cholesterol 105mg; Sodium 970mg; Total Carbohydrate 20g (Dietary Fiber 0g); Protein 32g **Exchanges:** 1½ Starch, 3 Very Lean Meat, 1 Lean Meat, 2 Fat **Carbohydrate Choices:** 1

Make It a Meal
Serve these nuggets with barbecue sauce, honey mustard or sweet-and-sour dipping sauce for a real treat.

Genius Tip
For easy dipping, use tongs to coat the chicken pieces on all sides with the butter and cereal mixtures.

Chicken and Dumplings

Prep Time: 20 Minutes • Start to Finish: 45 Minutes • 4 servings

CHICKEN

2½ cups gluten-free chicken broth (from 32-oz carton)

1½ cups cut-up cooked chicken

1 cup frozen mixed vegetables

1 teaspoon gluten-free seasoned salt

¼ teaspoon pepper

1 cup milk

3 tablespoons cornstarch

DUMPLINGS

¾ cup Bisquick® Gluten Free mix

⅓ cup milk

2 tablespoons butter, melted

1 egg

1 tablespoon chopped fresh parsley

1 In 3-quart saucepan, heat broth, chicken, vegetables, seasoned salt and pepper to boiling. In small bowl, mix 1 cup milk and the cornstarch with whisk until smooth. Stir cornstarch mixture into chicken mixture; heat just to boiling.

2 In small bowl, stir dumpling ingredients with fork until blended. Gently drop dough by 8 rounded spoonfuls onto boiling chicken mixture.

3 Cook uncovered over low heat 10 minutes. Cover; cook 15 minutes longer or until dumplings are completely cooked in center.

1 Serving: Calories 360; Total Fat 14g (Saturated Fat 6g, Trans Fat 0g); Cholesterol 120mg; Sodium 1390mg; Total Carbohydrate 36g (Dietary Fiber 2g); Protein 24g **Exchanges:** 1½ Starch, ½ Other Carbohydrate, ½ Vegetable, 2½ Lean Meat, 1 Fat **Carbohydrate Choices:** 2½

Make It a Meal For a family supper, serve the chicken and dumplings with a crisp, mixed-greens salad and gluten-free brownie sundaes

Skinny Mexican Chicken Casserole

Prep Time: 20 Minutes • Start to Finish: 1 Hour 5 Minutes • 8 servings

1 bag (10 oz) frozen whole-grain brown rice

1 bag (12 oz) frozen whole kernel sweet corn

1 can (15 oz) black beans, drained, rinsed

2 cups cubed cooked chicken breast

2 cans (10 oz each) enchilada sauce

1 cup chopped red bell pepper

¼ cup chopped green onions (4 medium)

¼ cup chopped fresh cilantro

1 teaspoon chili powder

½ teaspoon ground cumin

½ teaspoon garlic powder

2 cups shredded reduced-fat Mexican cheese blend (8 oz)

1 cup shredded lettuce

1 tomato, chopped

1 Heat oven to 375°F. Spray 13×9-inch (3-quart) glass baking dish with cooking spray. Cook rice and corn as directed on packages. In baking dish, carefully stir rice, corn, beans, chicken, enchilada sauce, bell pepper, 2 tablespoons of the green onions, the cilantro, chili powder, cumin, garlic powder and 1 cup of the cheese until well blended.

2 Bake uncovered 30 to 35 minutes or until bubbly and thoroughly heated. Sprinkle with remaining 1 cup cheese. Bake 3 minutes longer or until cheese is melted.

3 Top with shredded lettuce, tomato and remaining 2 tablespoons green onions.

1 Serving: Calories 300; Total Fat 8g (Saturated Fat 4g, Trans Fat 0g); Cholesterol 45mg; Sodium 720mg; Total Carbohydrate 33g (Dietary Fiber 6g); Protein 22g **Exchanges:** 2 Other Carbohydrate, ½ Vegetable, 2 Very Lean Meat, 1 Medium-Fat Meat, ½ Fat **Carbohydrate Choices:** 2

Genius Tip You can prepare the casserole up to a day ahead; cover and refrigerate. Bake as directed, adding about 5 minutes to bake time to compensate for the refrigeration.

Skinny Chicken and Black Bean Burritos

Prep Time: 25 Minutes • Start to Finish: 25 Minutes • 8 burritos

2 cups shredded cooked chicken breast

1 can (15 oz) black beans, drained, rinsed

1 cup chunky-style salsa

2 teaspoons chili powder

1 cup cooked instant brown rice

¼ cup chopped fresh cilantro

1 tablespoon lime juice

8 low-fat whole-wheat tortillas (8 inch)

1 cup shredded reduced-fat sharp Cheddar cheese

Chunky-style salsa, if desired

1 In medium microwavable bowl, mix chicken, black beans, 1 cup salsa and the chili powder. Microwave on High 2 minutes or until hot, stirring after 1 minute.

2 In large bowl, mix cooked rice, cilantro and lime juice until well blended.

3 Heat tortillas as directed on package. Spoon about ½ cup chicken mixture down center of each tortilla. Top with about ¼ cup rice mixture and 2 tablespoons cheese. Fold sides of tortilla toward center; fold ends over. Serve with additional salsa.

1 Burrito: Calories 240; Total Fat 8g (Saturated Fat 3.5g, Trans Fat 0g); Cholesterol 45mg; Sodium 430mg; Total Carbohydrate 23g (Dietary Fiber 5g); Protein 18g **Exchanges:** 1½ Starch, 2 Lean Meat, ½ Fat **Carbohydrate Choices:** 1½

Customize It Any type of beans can be used in place of the black beans, though smaller beans work best in burritos and wraps. Also, add a little more spice with additional chili powder and cilantro!

Herb Roast Chicken and Vegetables

Prep Time: 20 Minutes • Start to Finish: 2 Hours 5 Minutes • 6 servings

¼ cup olive or vegetable oil

2 tablespoons chopped fresh thyme leaves or 1 teaspoon dried thyme leaves

2 tablespoons chopped fresh marjoram leaves or 1 teaspoon dried marjoram leaves

½ teaspoon salt

¼ teaspoon coarsely ground pepper

1 lemon

1 whole roasting chicken (4 lb)

6 new potatoes, cut in half

1 cup ready-to-eat baby-cut carrots

8 oz fresh green beans

1 Heat oven to 375°F. In small bowl, mix oil, thyme, marjoram, salt and pepper. Grate 1 teaspoon peel from lemon; add peel to oil mixture. Cut lemon into quarters; place in cavity of chicken.

2 Fold wings of chicken across back with tips touching. Tie or skewer drumsticks to tail. Place chicken, breast side up, on rack in shallow roasting pan. Brush oil mixture on chicken. Insert meat thermometer in chicken so tip is in thickest part of inside thigh muscle and does not touch bone.

3 Roast uncovered 45 minutes. Arrange potatoes, carrots and green beans around chicken; brush chicken and vegetables with oil mixture. Roast uncovered 30 to 45 minutes or until thermometer reads 180°F and juice of chicken is no longer pink when center of thigh is cut. Let stand about 15 minutes for easiest carving. Remove lemon and discard.

4 Place chicken on platter; arrange vegetables around chicken. Serve with pan drippings.

1 Serving: Calories 460; Total Fat 27g (Saturated Fat 6g, Trans Fat 0.5g); Cholesterol 115mg; Sodium 330mg; Total Carbohydrate 16g (Dietary Fiber 3g); Protein 38g **Exchanges:** ½ Starch, ½ Other Carbohydrate, ½ Vegetable, 3 Very Lean Meat, 2 Lean Meat, 4 Fat **Carbohydrate Choices:** 1

Genius Tip For easy cleanup, line the pan with foil before placing the chicken on the rack in the pan.

Skinny Creamy Chicken Enchiladas

Prep Time: 30 Minutes • **Start to Finish: 1 Hour 10 Minutes** • **8 enchiladas**

ENCHILADAS

- 1 tablespoon olive oil
- ½ cup chopped onion (1 medium)
- 2 teaspoons finely chopped garlic
- 2 cups reduced-sodium chicken broth (from 32-oz carton)
- 3 tablespoons all-purpose flour
- ½ teaspoon ground coriander or cumin
- ⅛ teaspoon pepper
- ½ cup reduced-fat sour cream
- 2 cups shredded cooked chicken breast
- 1 cup frozen whole kernel corn, thawed
- 1 cup shredded reduced-fat Mexican cheese blend (4 oz)
- 1 can (4.5 oz) chopped green chiles
- ¼ cup chopped fresh cilantro
- 8 corn or flour tortillas (6 or 7 inch)

TOPPINGS

- 1 medium tomato, chopped (¾ cup)
- 4 medium green onions, sliced (¼ cup)
  Chunky-style salsa, if desired

1 Heat oven to 350°F. Spray 13×9-inch (3-quart) glass baking dish with cooking spray. In 10-inch nonstick skillet, heat oil over medium heat. Add onion and garlic; cook 3 to 4 minutes, stirring occasionally, until onion is tender.

2 In medium bowl, stir broth, flour, coriander and pepper with whisk until blended. Slowly add to hot mixture in skillet, stirring constantly. Cook and stir 5 to 6 minutes, until mixture boils and thickens slightly. Remove from heat. Stir in sour cream until well blended.

3 In another medium bowl, mix chicken, corn, ½ cup of the cheese, the chiles, cilantro and ½ cup of the sauce. Place 2 tortillas at a time on microwavable plate; cover with paper towel. Microwave on High 10 to 15 seconds or until softened. Spoon about ⅓ cup chicken mixture down center of each warm tortilla. Roll up tortillas; arrange, seam sides down, in baking dish. Top enchiladas with remaining sauce. Cover with foil.

4 Bake 30 to 35 minutes or until sauce is bubbly. Remove from oven. Uncover; sprinkle with remaining ½ cup cheese. Let stand 5 minutes before serving. Just before serving, top with tomato and green onions. Serve with salsa.

1 Enchilada: Calories 240; Total Fat 9g (Saturated Fat 3.5g, Trans Fat 0g); Cholesterol 45mg; Sodium 370mg; Total Carbohydrate 22g (Dietary Fiber 2g); Protein 17g **Exchanges:** 1 Other Carbohydrate, 1 Vegetable, 1½ Very Lean Meat, ½ Lean Meat, 1½ Fat **Carbohydrate Choices:** 1½

Customize It Reduced-fat mild or sharp Cheddar cheese can be substituted for the Mexican blend.

Genius Tip Heating the tortillas until they are soft enough to roll helps prevent them from cracking.

Stuffed Chicken Parmesan

Prep Time: 25 Minutes • Start to Finish: 1 Hour • 6 servings

6 boneless skinless chicken breasts (1¾ lb)

1 box (10 oz) frozen cut spinach, thawed, well drained

2 oz ⅓-less-fat cream cheese (Neufchâtel), softened

¼ cup shredded Parmesan cheese (1 oz)

1½ teaspoons dried basil leaves

1 clove garlic, finely chopped

¼ cup fat-free egg product

12 stone-ground wheat crackers, crushed (about ½ cup)

½ teaspoon pepper

1 cup Italian herb tomato pasta sauce

¼ cup shredded mozzarella cheese (1 oz)

1 Heat oven to 375°F. Spray 13×9-inch (3-quart) glass baking dish with cooking spray. Between sheets of plastic wrap or waxed paper, place each chicken breast, smooth side down. Gently pound with flat side of meat mallet or rolling pin until about ¼ inch thick.

2 In medium bowl, mix spinach, cream cheese, Parmesan cheese, ½ teaspoon of the basil and the garlic until blended. Spread about 1 tablespoon spinach mixture over each chicken breast; roll up tightly. If necessary, secure with toothpicks.

3 Into shallow bowl, pour egg product. In another shallow bowl, mix cracker crumbs, pepper and remaining 1 teaspoon basil. Dip each chicken breast into egg product; coat with crumb mixture. Place, seam side down, in baking dish.

4 Bake uncovered 20 minutes. Pour pasta sauce over chicken; sprinkle with mozzarella cheese. Bake 10 to 15 minutes longer or until chicken is no longer pink in center. Remove toothpicks before serving.

1 Serving: Calories 330; Total Fat 13g (Saturated Fat 4.5g, Trans Fat 0g); Cholesterol 115mg; Sodium 440mg; Total Carbohydrate 9g (Dietary Fiber 2g); Protein 44g **Exchanges:** ½ Starch, 5½ Very Lean Meat, ½ Medium-Fat Meat, 1½ Fat **Carbohydrate Choices:** ½

Cheesy Chicken and Tortilla Chip Casserole

Prep Time: 15 Minutes • Start to Finish: 50 Minutes • 8 servings

1 bag (10 oz) ranch-flavored tortilla chips, coarsely crushed (about 6 cups)

¼ cup butter, melted

2 cups shredded Colby–Monterey Jack cheese (8 oz)

1 jar (15 oz) four-cheese Alfredo pasta sauce

1 tablespoon original taco seasoning mix (from 1-oz package)

3 cups shredded cooked chicken

1 can (14.5 oz) fire-roasted diced tomatoes, undrained

1 Heat oven to 350°F. Spray 13×9-inch (3-quart) glass baking dish with cooking spray. In large bowl, toss tortilla chips and melted butter until well coated. Sprinkle 4 cups of the tortilla chips evenly in bottom of casserole. Top with ½ cup of the cheese.

2 In large bowl, stir pasta sauce and taco seasoning mix until well blended. Add chicken, tomatoes and ½ cup of the cheese; stir until well mixed. Spoon evenly over tortilla chips in baking dish.

3 Bake uncovered 30 minutes. Sprinkle with remaining tortilla chips and remaining 1 cup cheese. Bake about 5 minutes longer or until hot and cheese is melted.

1 Serving: Calories 640; Total Fat 45g (Saturated Fat 22g, Trans Fat 1g); Cholesterol 140mg; Sodium 850mg; Total Carbohydrate 30g (Dietary Fiber 2g); Protein 27g **Exchanges:** 1 Starch, 1 Other Carbohydrate, 2½ Lean Meat, 1 High-Fat Meat, 6 Fat **Carbohydrate Choices:** 2

Genius Tip Use any of your favorite flavored tortilla chips in this recipe.

Genius Tip Rotisserie chicken works well for this recipe. Boned and preshredded can be found in the deli section of your favorite grocery store.

Chicken Noodle Soup

Prep Time: 15 Minutes • Start to Finish: 25 Minutes • 4 servings

1 tablespoon olive or vegetable oil

2 cloves garlic, finely chopped

8 medium green onions, sliced (½ cup)

2 medium carrots, chopped (1 cup)

2 cups cubed cooked chicken

2 cups uncooked egg noodles (4 oz)

1 tablespoon chopped fresh parsley or 1 teaspoon parsley flakes

¼ teaspoon pepper

1 dried bay leaf

5¼ cups chicken broth (from two 32-oz cartons)

1 In 3-quart saucepan, heat oil over medium heat. Add garlic, onions and carrots; cook 4 minutes, stirring occasionally.

2 Stir in remaining ingredients. Heat to boiling; reduce heat.

3 Cover; simmer about 10 minutes, stirring occasionally, until carrots and noodles are tender. Remove bay leaf.

1 Serving: Calories 290; Total Fat 12g (Saturated Fat 2.5g, Trans Fat 0.5g); Cholesterol 85mg; Sodium 1520mg; Total Carbohydrate 21g (Dietary Fiber 2g); Protein 25g **Exchanges:** 1 Starch, ½ Vegetable, 2 Very Lean Meat, 1 Medium-Fat Meat, 1 Fat **Carbohydrate Choices:** 1½

Impossibly Easy Chicken and Broccoli Pie

2 cups frozen cut broccoli, thawed, drained

1½ cups shredded Cheddar cheese (6 oz)

1 cup cut-up cooked chicken or 2 cans (5 oz each) chunk chicken, well drained

1 medium onion, chopped (½ cup)

½ cup Original Bisquick® mix

1 cup milk

½ teaspoon salt

¼ teaspoon pepper

2 eggs

1 Heat oven to 400°F. Spray 9-inch glass pie plate with cooking spray. Sprinkle broccoli, 1 cup of the cheese, the chicken and onion in pie plate.

2 In medium bowl, stir remaining ingredients with whisk or fork until blended. Pour over mixture in pie plate.

3 Bake 35 to 38 minutes or until knife inserted in center comes out clean. Sprinkle with remaining ½ cup cheese. Bake 1 to 2 minutes longer or until cheese is melted. Let stand 5 minutes before serving.

1 Serving: Calories 230; Total Fat 13g (Saturated Fat 6g, Trans Fat 0g); Cholesterol 95mg; Sodium 530mg; Total Carbohydrate 12g (Dietary Fiber 1g); Protein 15g **Exchanges:** 1 Other Carbohydrate, 1 Very Lean Meat, 1 High-Fat Meat, 1 Fat **Carbohydrate Choices:** 1

Genius Tip This supper pie can be covered and refrigerated up to 24 hours before baking. You may need to bake a bit longer than the recipe directs since you'll be starting with a cold pie. Watch carefully for doneness.

Pesto Pasta with Chicken and Tomatoes

Prep Time: 15 Minutes • Start to Finish: 30 Minutes • 6 servings (1½ cups each)

PESTO

- 1 cup firmly packed fresh basil leaves
- ⅓ cup grated Parmesan cheese
- ¼ cup olive oil
- 1 clove garlic
- 2 tablespoons sliced almonds, toasted

PASTA

- 12 oz uncooked penne pasta (3½ cups)
- 3 cups chicken broth (from 32-oz carton)
- 2 cups shredded cooked chicken
- 2 cups halved cherry tomatoes
- ¼ cup julienne-cut fresh basil leaves
- 3 tablespoons grated Parmesan cheese

1 In blender or food processor, place all pesto ingredients. Cover; process on medium speed about 3 minutes or until smooth, stopping occasionally to scrape down sides with rubber spatula. Set aside.

2 In 4-quart saucepan, heat penne and broth just to boiling over high heat. Reduce heat to medium; cover and cook 8 to 10 minutes, stirring frequently, until pasta is tender and liquid is almost absorbed. Remove from heat. Stir in pesto, chicken and tomatoes. Cook over medium heat 2 to 3 minutes or until thoroughly heated.

3 Garnish with basil and 3 tablespoons Parmesan cheese.

1 Serving: Calories 480; Total Fat 19g (Saturated Fat 4.5g, Trans Fat 0g); Cholesterol 45mg; Sodium 740mg; Total Carbohydrate 52g (Dietary Fiber 4g); Protein 27g **Exchanges:** 2 Starch, 1 Other Carbohydrate, 1 Vegetable, 2½ Lean Meat, 2 Fat **Carbohydrate Choices:** 3½

Genius Tip For a quick and easy way to julienne-cut basil leaves, stack the leaves, roll them up tightly lengthwise and cut into thin strips, starting from one end and cutting to the other.

Make It a Meal For a lovely meal, serve with a crispy green salad and crusty loaf of bread.

Moroccan Chicken with Olives

Prep Time: 25 Minutes • Start to Finish: 1 Hour 25 Minutes • 6 servings

¼ cup chopped
   fresh cilantro

1 tablespoon paprika

2 teaspoons ground cumin

½ teaspoon salt

½ teaspoon ground
   turmeric

½ teaspoon ground ginger

2 garlic cloves, finely
   chopped

1 cut-up whole chicken
   (3 to 3½ lb)

⅓ cup all-purpose flour

½ cup water

¼ cup lemon juice

1 teaspoon chicken
   bouillon granules

½ cup Kalamata or
   Greek olives

1 medium lemon, sliced

   Hot cooked couscous
   or rice, if desired

1 Heat oven to 350°F. In small bowl, mix cilantro, paprika, cumin, salt, turmeric, ginger and garlic. Rub mixture on all sides of chicken pieces.

2 Place flour in shallow dish. Coat all sides of chicken pieces with flour. Place chicken in 13×9-inch (3-quart) glass baking dish. In small bowl, mix water, lemon juice and bouillon granules; pour over chicken in baking dish. Add olives and lemon slices.

3 Bake uncovered 55 to 65 minutes, occasionally spooning liquid in baking dish over chicken, until juice of chicken is no longer pink when centers of thickest pieces are cut to bone (165°F). Serve with couscous.

1 Serving: Calories 290; Total Fat 15g (Saturated Fat 4g, Trans Fat 0g); Cholesterol 85mg; Sodium 500mg; Total Carbohydrate 9g (Dietary Fiber 1g); Protein 28g **Exchanges:** ½ Starch, 3½ Very Lean Meat, 2½ Fat **Carbohydrate Choices:** ½

Genius Tip Turmeric is an aromatic spice with a brilliant yellow color and a pungent, slightly bitter flavor. Often used in Indian and Caribbean cooking, turmeric is commonly added to poultry, rice, seafood and egg dishes.

Customize It Kalamata olives garnish this Moroccan dish to add a slightly salty flavor. Greek or even ripe olives can be used if you can't get Kalamata olives.

Make It a Meal Dress up this dish for entertaining when you serve it beside couscous with raisins and Middle Eastern flatbread.

Chicken Sausage and Mini Pepper Pizza

Prep Time: 10 Minutes • Start to Finish: 20 Minutes • 4 servings

1 package (14 oz) prebaked thin Italian pizza crust (12 inch)

½ cup salsa verde (from 16-oz jar)

1 pineapple-bacon chicken sausage link, thinly sliced (from 12-oz package)

3 miniature bell peppers (from 1-lb bag), cut into rings

1 tablespoon chopped fresh cilantro

1 cup shredded Colby– Monterey Jack cheese blend (4 oz)

1 Heat oven to 450°F. On ungreased cookie sheet or 14-inch pizza pan, place pizza crust. Spread salsa verde over crust to within ½ inch of edge.

2 Arrange chicken sausage slices and pepper rings over pizza crust; sprinkle with cilantro. Top with cheese.

3 Bake 9 to 11 minutes or until cheese is melted and pizza is thoroughly heated. To serve, cut into 8 wedges.

1 Serving: Calories 460; Total Fat 19g (Saturated Fat 6g, Trans Fat 0g); Cholesterol 45mg; Sodium 980mg; Total Carbohydrate 55g (Dietary Fiber 1g); Protein 17g **Exchanges:** 3 Starch, ½ Other Carbohydrate, ½ Vegetable, 1 High-Fat Meat, 2 Fat **Carbohydrate Choices:** 3½

Customize It If you like sausage in every bite, cut the sausage slices in half. With so many flavor options for cooked chicken sausage, it might be fun to try other flavors for a different twist on this easy pizza.

Genius Tip Miniature peppers are a hybrid sweet pepper known for their sweet taste and crisp texture. We loved the unique flavor of this pizza that came from these little cuties. It's a little different from regular bell peppers. You will find them in a trio of colors (orange, red and yellow) in 1-pound packages.

Garlic-Lime Flank Steak Fajitas

Prep Time: 40 Minutes • Start to Finish: 40 Minutes • 6 servings

FAJITAS

1⅓ lb beef flank steak, trimmed of visible fat

1 package (1 oz) original taco seasoning mix

1 tablespoon packed brown sugar

1 tablespoon finely chopped garlic

¼ teaspoon ground red pepper (cayenne)

¼ cup lime juice

2 large red or yellow bell peppers, cut into ¼-inch strips (about 3 cups)

1 cup sliced onion

1 tablespoon vegetable oil

1 teaspoon ground cumin

1 teaspoon ground coriander

½ teaspoon salt

6 flour tortillas for burritos (8 inch; from 11.5-oz package), heated as directed on package

TOPPINGS, IF DESIRED

Chopped fresh cilantro

Sliced green onions

Sliced avocado

Sour cream

Lime slices

1 Place beef in large, resealable food-storage plastic bag. In small bowl, mix taco seasoning mix, brown sugar, garlic, ground red pepper and lime juice. Pour mixture over beef. Seal bag; refrigerate 8 to 10 hours.

2 In medium bowl, mix bell peppers, onion, oil, cumin, coriander and salt; set aside.

3 Spray 12- to 13-inch round grill pan with cooking spray; heat over medium-high heat. Remove beef from marinade; place in pan. Discard any remaining marinade.

4 Cook 10 to 20 minutes, turning once, until instant-read thermometer inserted in thickest part of steak reads 135°F (for medium). Transfer steak to cutting board; tent with foil, and let stand 5 minutes.

5 Meanwhile, in grill pan, cook pepper and onion mixture 5 to 7 minutes, stirring occasionally, until vegetables are crisp-tender and browned.

6 Cut steak across grain at angle into thin slices. To serve, place beef and vegetables down center of warmed tortillas. Top with remaining ingredients.

1 Serving: Calories 330; Total Fat 10g (Saturated Fat 3g, Trans Fat 1g); Cholesterol 65mg; Sodium 900mg; Total Carbohydrate 32g (Dietary Fiber 2g); Protein 28g **Exchanges:** 2 Starch, 1 Vegetable, 3 Lean Meat **Carbohydrate Choices:** 2

Genius Tip Flank steak varies in thickness. For best doneness results, select a steak that is an even thickness throughout.

Supper Solution:
Let's Oven-Fry!

Oven-frying is an easy way to get your meal on the table! It's a terrific way to add flavor and texture with little fuss. If you have a convection oven, this is a great place to use it. The circulating air helps to crisp the outsides of oven-fried foods. Cleanup is a breeze when you line your pan with foil. It helps the food brown and then can be wrapped up and thrown out.

FOLLOW THE DIRECTIONS BELOW FOR SPECIFIC FOODS USING THESE GUIDELINES:

Heat oven as directed below. Line cookie sheet with foil; spray with cooking spray.

Mix dry coating ingredients with the desired seasoning ingredients in a shallow dish or large resealable food-storage bag (see below).

Place wet coating ingredients in another shallow dish.

Dip food in wet coating ingredients then into dry coating ingredients, coating both sides and pressing into the food. (Use one hand for dipping foods into the wet ingredients, the other hand for dipping into the dry ingredients to keep your hands from accumulating too much of the coating ingredients on them.)

Drizzle with ¼ cup melted butter over the coated food on the pan, or spray with baking spray to help with browning and crispness.

Bake uncovered as directed.

FOOD	OVEN TEMPERATURE	DIRECTIONS
Fish fillets, *cut into serving pieces*	400°F or 425°F	Bake until fish flakes easily with a fork.

Chicken
Cut-up pieces (bone-in)
    Breast halves
Chicken fingers or tenders
    (about 1½-inch strips)
Wings
	425°F	Bone-in Pieces Doneness: Bake until juice of chicken is clear when thickest piece is cut to bone and thermometer inserted in thickest part (not touching bone) reads at least 165°F.
		How-To: Place, skin side down, in pan. Bake 30 minutes; turn pieces skin side up. Bake about 20 minutes longer.
		Boneless Pieces Doneness: Bake until chicken is no longer pink when cut in center.
		How-To: Bake 15 minutes; turn. Bake 10 to 15 minutes longer.

Veggies Whole button mushrooms, zucchini slices *(½ inch thick)* or bell pepper strips	400°F	Arrange in single layer on greased cookie sheet. Bake 10 minutes; turn. Bake 10 minutes longer or until golden brown.
Potatoes, cut into wedges	425°F	Pick only a seasoning (do not use dry and wet coating ingredients). Don't use butter. **Bake** about 25 minutes, turning once, or until golden brown on both sides.
Pork chops, boneless or bone-in (½ inch thick)	425°F	**Bake** 30 to 35 minutes until no longer pink in center and meat thermometer inserted in center reaches 145°F.

CUSTOMIZABLE COATINGS (FOR 4 TO 6 SERVINGS)

Mix and Match: Pick a dry coating, seasoning and wet coating, mixing all ingredients together for each type. Follow directions on page 291.

PICK A DRY COATING	PICK A SEASONING	PICK A WET COATING
All-Purpose ½ cup all-purpose flour or Original Bisquick®	**Herb Seasoning** ¼ teaspoon dried herbs (such as dill weed, basil, thyme, oregano or rosemary leaves) ½ teaspoon paprika ¼ teaspoon salt ⅛ teaspoon pepper	1 egg + 2 tablespoons water or milk, beaten
Crunchy Cornmeal ¼ cup cornmeal + ¼ cup dry bread crumbs	**Savory Seasoning** 1 teaspoon seasoned salt 1 teaspoon paprika ½ teaspoon garlic powder ¼ teaspoon pepper	½ cup creamy Caesar or Italian salad dressing
Crispy Parmesan ½ cup panko crispy bread crumbs + ¼ cup shredded Parmesan cheese + ½ cup finely ground toasted sliced or slivered almonds (if desired)	**Lemon-Pepper Seasoning** 1 teaspoon Italian seasoning 1 teaspoon lemon-pepper seasoning	¾ cup regular or reduced-fat ranch dressing
Cheesy Cracker ¾ to 1½ cups crushed crackers or chips ½ cup finely shredded cheese	**Spicy Seasoning** ¼ teaspoon salt ¼ teaspoon garlic powder ¼ teaspoon dried oregano leaves ¼ to ½ teaspoon ground red pepper (cayenne) ¼ teaspoon pepper	½ cup milk or buttermilk

Impossibly Easy Pizza Bake

Prep Time: 15 Minutes • Start to Finish: 35 Minutes • 8 servings

3⅓ cups Original Bisquick® mix

1 cup milk

1 jar (14 oz) pizza sauce

1 package (7 oz) sliced pepperoni

1 bag (8 oz) shredded mozzarella cheese (2 cups)

1 Heat oven to 375°F. Spray 13×9-inch (3-quart) glass baking dish with cooking spray. In medium bowl, stir Bisquick mix and milk until soft dough forms. Drop half of dough by spoonfuls evenly in bottom of baking dish (dough will not completely cover bottom of dish).

2 Drizzle about 1 cup pizza sauce over dough. Arrange half of the pepperoni slices evenly over sauce. Top with 1 cup of the cheese. Repeat layers with remaining dough, pizza sauce, pepperoni and cheese.

3 Bake 25 to 30 minutes or until golden brown, biscuits in center are cooked and cheese in center is bubbly.

1 Serving: Calories 450; Total Fat 24g (Saturated Fat 9g, Trans Fat 2.5g); Cholesterol 45mg; Sodium 1310mg; Total Carbohydrate 39g (Dietary Fiber 2g); Protein 18g **Exchanges:** 1 Starch, 1 Other Carbohydrate, 1 Vegetable, 1 Lean Meat, 1 High-Fat Meat, 2½ Fat **Carbohydrate Choices:** 2½

Customize It To make half of the recipe, divide ingredients in half; bake in sprayed 8-inch square (2-quart) glass baking dish 22 to 25 minutes.

Customize It Add your favorite pizza toppings to the layers. Try cooked sausage crumbles, chopped green bell pepper, onion or olives.

Genius Tip This easy recipe can be covered and refrigerated up to 24 hours before baking. You may need to bake a bit longer than the recipe directs since you'll be starting with a cold pie. Watch carefully for doneness.

Ravioli and Chorizo Packets

Prep Time: 15 Minutes • Start to Finish: 35 Minutes • 4 packets

¼ cup creamy balsamic vinaigrette or zesty Italian dressing

¼ teaspoon garlic powder

¼ teaspoon pepper

4 smoked chorizo sausage links (12 oz), cut crosswise into quarters

1 cup frozen miniature cheese-filled ravioli (about 5 oz)

1 cup grape tomatoes, halved

1 medium zucchini, cut into 3x½-inch strips

1 tablespoon chopped fresh parsley

1 Heat oven to 350°F. Cut 4 (18x12-inch) sheets of heavy-duty foil. In medium bowl, mix vinaigrette, garlic powder and pepper with whisk. Add chorizo, ravioli, tomatoes and zucchini; toss to coat.

2 Place equal amounts of sausage mixture in center of each sheet of foil. Bring up 2 sides of foil so edges meet. Seal edges, making ½-inch fold; fold again, allowing space for heat circulation and expansion. Place packets on large cookie sheet.

3 Bake 15 to 20 minutes or until the pasta is tender. Carefully unfold packets; sprinkle with parsley.

1 Packet: Calories 520; Total Fat 40g (Saturated Fat 14g, Trans Fat 0g); Cholesterol 110mg; Sodium 1410mg; Total Carbohydrate 15g (Dietary Fiber 1g); Protein 25g **Exchanges:** 1 Starch, ½ Vegetable, 3 High-Fat Meat, 3 Fat **Carbohydrate Choices:** 1

Customize It You can use almost any other cooked or smoked link sausage, such as Polish sausage, andouille, bratwurst or chicken sausage in these packets.

Genius Tip The frozen ravioli cooks up perfectly in these packets, but if you want to use a different frozen pasta, be sure it's about the same size as miniature ravioli. Large ravioli may not get completely done when the veggies are done.

Taco Dog Potato Nugget Casserole

Prep Time: 20 Minutes • Start to Finish: 1 Hour 10 Minutes • 6 servings (1½ cups each)

1 lb lean (at least 80%) ground beef

1 large onion, chopped (1 cup)

1 package (1 oz) reduced-sodium taco seasoning mix

1 can (14.5 oz) diced tomatoes with green chiles, undrained

3 hot dogs, cut in half lengthwise, then crosswise into ½-inch pieces

1 can (10½ oz) condensed cream of onion soup

1 package (8 oz) shredded Mexican cheese blend

1 package (28 oz) frozen miniature potato nuggets

Chopped fresh cilantro and sliced green onions, if desired

1 Heat oven to 350°F. Spray 13×9-inch (3-quart) glass baking dish with cooking spray. In 12-inch nonstick skillet, cook beef and onion over medium-high heat 7 to 9 minutes, stirring frequently, until brown. Drain. Reduce heat to medium.

2 Stir in 2 tablespoons of the taco seasoning mix, the tomatoes and hot dogs. Cook and stir until thoroughly heated. Stir in soup and 1 cup of the shredded cheese until melted.

3 Place half (about 3½ cups) of the frozen potatoes in single layer in baking dish; spoon beef mixture on top. In large resealable food-storage plastic bag, combine remaining potatoes and remaining taco seasoning mix; seal bag and shake to coat. Arrange seasoned potatoes on top of casserole (discard any remaining taco seasoning mix left in bag).

4 Bake uncovered 40 minutes. Top casserole with remaining 1 cup cheese. Bake 3 to 5 minutes or until cheese is melted and potatoes are lightly browned. Top with cilantro and green onions.

1 Serving: Calories 670; Total Fat 40g (Saturated Fat 15g, Trans Fat 5g); Cholesterol 100mg; Sodium 1660mg; Total Carbohydrate 50g (Dietary Fiber 4g); Protein 28g **Exchanges:** 2 Starch, 1½ Other Carbohydrate, 2 Medium-Fat Meat, 1 High-Fat Meat, 4 Fat **Carbohydrate Choices:** 3

Make It a Meal Serve with your favorite taco toppings like sour cream or salsa.

Tuna Melt-Tot Bake

Prep Time: 20 Minutes • Start to Finish: 50 Minutes • 6 servings (about 1 cup each)

2 tablespoons butter

2 tablespoons all-purpose flour

¼ teaspoon salt

⅛ teaspoon pepper

1½ cups milk

1¼ cups shredded sharp Cheddar cheese (5 oz)

1½ cups grape tomatoes, halved

2 stalks celery, chopped (about ⅔ cup)

4 medium green onions, sliced (¼ cup)

1 can (12 oz) albacore tuna in water, drained

½ package (28 oz) frozen miniature potato nuggets (about 3½ cups)

Chopped fresh parsley, if desired

1 Heat oven to 350°F. Spray 11×7-inch (2-quart) glass baking dish with cooking spray. In 3-quart saucepan, melt butter over low heat. Stir in flour, salt and pepper. Cook over low heat, stirring constantly, until mixture is smooth and bubbly.

2 Gradually stir in milk with whisk. Heat to boiling, stirring constantly. Boil and stir 1 minute. Stir in 1 cup of the cheese until melted. Stir in tomatoes, celery, green onions and tuna until mixed.

3 Pour tuna mixture into baking dish; top with potato nuggets.

4 Bake 20 to 25 minutes or until potato nuggets are golden brown. Sprinkle with remaining ¼ cup cheese; bake about 2 minutes longer or until cheese is melted. Let stand 5 minutes. Garnish with parsley.

1 Serving: Calories 380; Total Fat 21g (Saturated Fat 9g, Trans Fat 3g); Cholesterol 60mg; Sodium 830mg; Total Carbohydrate 27g (Dietary Fiber 2g); Protein 22g **Exchanges:** 1½ Other Carbohydrate, 1 Vegetable, 2 Lean Meat, 1 High-Fat Meat, 1½ Fat **Carbohydrate Choices:** 2

Customize It You can substitute 1¼ cups chopped cooked chicken for the tuna.

Genius Tip When making the cheesy white sauce, be sure to bring the mixture to a boil while stirring constantly to avoid any burning. Boiling it for an additional 1 minute helps to remove any flour taste in the sauce.

Jalapeño Tuna and Zucchini Lasagna

Prep Time: 25 Minutes • Start to Finish: 1 Hour 20 Minutes • 6 servings

2 medium zucchini, cut lengthwise into ⅛-inch slices

2 teaspoons salt

1 package (8 oz) cream cheese, softened

½ cup mayonnaise

¼ cup sour cream

1½ cups frozen roasted whole kernel corn, thawed

1 medium jalapeño chile, seeded, finely chopped

½ teaspoon Sriracha sauce

2 cans (5 oz each) tuna in water, drained

1 jar (2 oz) diced pimientos, drained

½ cup plain panko crispy bread crumbs

2 cups shredded pepper Jack cheese (8 oz)

2 tablespoons fresh cilantro leaves

1 Place zucchini on paper towel–lined tray. Sprinkle zucchini with 1 teaspoon of the salt; let stand 10 minutes. Turn zucchini over; sprinkle with remaining salt. Let stand 10 minutes. Rinse; pat dry with paper towel.

2 Meanwhile, in medium bowl, mix cream cheese, mayonnaise and sour cream until well mixed. Gently stir in corn, jalapeño chile, Sriracha sauce, tuna and pimientos.

3 Heat oven to 350°F. Spray 11×7-inch (2-quart) glass baking dish with cooking spray. Spread 1 cup of the tuna mixture in bottom of baking dish. Sprinkle with 2 tablespoons of the bread crumbs. Layer with half of the zucchini. Spread remaining tuna mixture over zucchini slices; top with 1 cup of the pepper Jack cheese. Sprinkle with 2 tablespoons of the bread crumbs. Arrange remaining zucchini over bread crumbs. Sprinkle with the remaining 1 cup pepper Jack cheese and the bread crumbs. Spray foil with cooking spray; cover baking dish tightly with foil, sprayed side down.

4 Bake 35 minutes. Remove foil; bake an additional 10 to 15 minutes or until top is light golden brown. Let stand about 10 minutes before serving. Sprinkle with cilantro.

1 Serving: Calories 560; Total Fat 43g (Saturated Fat 19g, Trans Fat 1g); Cholesterol 105mg; Sodium 1450mg; Total Carbohydrate 20g (Dietary Fiber 2g); Protein 24g **Exchanges:** 1 Starch, 1 Vegetable, 2 Very Lean Meat, 1 High-Fat Meat, 6½ Fat **Carbohydrate Choices:** 1

Genius Tip If you own a mandoline, use it to cut nice, thin slices of the zucchini! Zucchini releases water during cooking. Salting the zucchini slices before assembling the lasagna pulls out excess moisture so the lasagna won't be watery when baked. Be sure to rinse the slices and pat them dry to avoid making the dish too salty.

Genius Tip Stocking your kitchen pantry with a box of disposable plastic gloves comes in handy when seeding and chopping jalapeño chiles, since they contain oils that can irritate the skin during chopping. If you touch other parts of your body with these oils, you can irritate them as well. So, wearing gloves eliminates the possibility of this happening.

Salmon and Whole-Grain Medley Packets

Prep Time: 25 Minutes • Start to Finish: 45 Minutes • 4 servings

1 pouch (8.5 oz) whole-grain medley ready rice

1 cup matchstick-cut carrots (from 10-oz bag)

1 small zucchini, cut into ½-inch cubes

2 small cloves garlic, finely chopped

¾ teaspoon salt

¼ teaspoon crushed red pepper flakes, if desired

¼ cup chopped fresh chives

1 lb salmon fillet, cut into 4 pieces

2 teaspoons olive oil

¼ teaspoon pepper

Lemon wedges, if desired

1 Heat oven to 375°F. Cut 4 (16×15-inch) pieces cooking parchment paper. Fold longest side of each piece in half lengthwise; crease and unfold. Spray each piece with cooking spray to within 1 inch of edges.

2 In large bowl, mix rice, carrots, zucchini, garlic, ¼ teaspoon of the salt, the crushed red pepper flakes and half of the chives. Spoon mixture evenly on half of each piece of parchment near center. Brush salmon fillet pieces with olive oil; sprinkle with remaining ½ teaspoon salt and the pepper; place on top of rice mixture.

3 Fold parchment paper over salmon and rice mixture. To seal edge of each packet, start at 1 end of open edges, fold paper over tightly 3 or 4 times, rotating and making small triangle-like folds to round edges of packet and folding packet edge under at end. (Packets should resemble half-moon shape and measure 11×5½ inches.)

4 Place packets on large cookie sheet. Bake 15 to 18 minutes, or until fish flakes easily with fork and vegetables are tender.

5 Let packets stand 5 minutes before serving. To serve, cut large X across top of each packet; carefully fold back points to allow steam to escape. Garnish with remaining chives and serve with lemon wedges.

1 Serving: Calories 370; Total Fat 15g (Saturated Fat 2.5g, Trans Fat 0g); Cholesterol 55mg; Sodium 530mg; Total Carbohydrate 35g (Dietary Fiber 2g); Protein 23g **Exchanges:** ½ Starch, 1½ Other Carbohydrate, ½ Vegetable, 3 Medium-Fat Meat **Carbohydrate Choices:** 2

Genius Tip Parchment paper is sold in rolls and is readily available in the grocery store. You may also substitute foil in place of parchment.

Make It a Meal Want to treat yourself? Serve this delicious meal with a side of crusty bread or a nice glass of white wine.

Sweet Potato–Black Bean Lasagna

Prep Time: 30 Minutes • Start to Finish: 1 Hour 25 Minutes • 6 servings

- 2 large red garnet sweet potatoes (about 2 lb)
- 1½ cups coarsely chopped broccoli
- 1 tablespoon water
- 2¼ cups roasted garlic Alfredo sauce
- 1 clove garlic, finely chopped
- ¼ cup chopped fresh basil leaves
- 6 oven-ready lasagna noodles
- 1 teaspoon garlic salt
- ½ teaspoon pepper
- 1 can (15 oz) black beans, drained, rinsed
- 1 medium red bell pepper, coarsely chopped (about ¾ cup)
- 2 cups finely shredded Italian cheese blend (8 oz)

1 Heat oven to 350°F. Spray 11×7-inch (2-quart) glass baking dish with cooking spray. Pierce sweet potatoes with fork. Place on paper towel in microwave oven.

2 Microwave on High 9 to 11 minutes or until slightly soft to the touch. Cool 15 minutes. Peel sweet potatoes; cut lengthwise into ¼-inch slices.

3 Meanwhile, in 1-quart microwavable bowl, place broccoli and water; cover loosely with plastic wrap. Microwave on High about 2 minutes or until crisp-tender. Immediately rinse and drain with cold water. Set aside.

4 In medium bowl, combine Alfredo sauce, garlic and 3 tablespoons of the basil until well mixed. Set aside.

5 Place 3 noodles in bottom of baking dish; spread ½ cup of the Alfredo sauce evenly over noodles. Layer half of the sweet potatoes over noodles, sprinkle with ½ teaspoon of the garlic salt and ¼ teaspoon of the pepper. Top potatoes with broccoli, beans and ½ cup of the bell pepper; sprinkle with 1 cup of the cheese. Top with remaining noodles, ¾ cup of the Alfredo sauce, remaining sweet potatoes, remaining ½ teaspoon garlic salt and ¼ teaspoon pepper. Spoon remaining sauce evenly over potatoes. Sprinkle with remaining bell pepper and cheese. Spray sheet of foil with cooking spray. Cover baking dish tightly with foil, sprayed side down.

6 Bake, covered, 40 to 45 minutes or until hot and cheese is melted. Remove foil; sprinkle with remaining basil. Let stand 15 minutes before serving.

1 Serving: Calories 710; Total Fat 38g (Saturated Fat 23g, Trans Fat 1g); Cholesterol 120mg; Sodium 1080mg; Total Carbohydrate 67g (Dietary Fiber 11g); Protein 23g **Exchanges:** 2 Starch, 2 Other Carbohydrate, 1½ Vegetable, 1 Very Lean Meat, 1 High-Fat Meat, 5½ Fat **Carbohydrate Choices:** 4½

Find It Look for precooked oven-ready lasagna noodles near the dry pasta in the grocery store or in the frozen pasta section. Trim the precooked lasagna noodles to fit your dish, if necessary.

Genius Tip Cooking the broccoli and immediately rinsing in cold water stops the cooking process so that when the lasagna is baked, the broccoli will still have its bright green color.

Impossibly Easy Roasted Peppers and Feta Cheese Pie

Prep Time: 20 Minutes • Start to Finish: 1 Hour • 6 servings

12 slices bacon, crisply cooked, crumbled

4 medium green onions, sliced (¼ cup)

⅓ cup chopped roasted red bell peppers, drained

½ cup crumbled feta cheese

¾ cup Original Bisquick® mix

1 cup milk

1 teaspoon dried basil leaves

3 eggs

1 Heat oven to 400°F. Spray 9-inch glass pie plate with cooking spray. In pie plate, mix bacon, onions and bell peppers. Sprinkle with cheese.

2 In medium bowl, mix remaining ingredients. Pour over mixture in pie plate.

3 Bake 30 to 35 minutes or until knife inserted in center comes out clean. Cool 5 minutes.

1 Serving: Calories 230; Total Fat 13g (Saturated Fat 6g, Trans Fat 0g); Cholesterol 125mg; Sodium 580mg; Total Carbohydrate 15g (Dietary Fiber 0g); Protein 13g **Exchanges:** 1 Starch, 1 Very Lean Meat, ½ Medium-Fat Meat, 2 Fat **Carbohydrate Choices:** 1

Genius Tip You're frying anyway, so why not fry a double batch of bacon and store the extra in your freezer? Having fried bacon on hand is great for sandwiches, seasoning vegetables or even reheated for breakfast!

Genius Tip This delicious pie can be covered and refrigerated up to 24 hours before baking. You may need to bake a bit longer than the recipe directs since you'll be starting with a cold pie. Watch carefully for doneness.

Impossibly Easy Vegetable Pie

Prep Time: 20 Minutes • Start to Finish: 1 Hour 5 Minutes • 6 servings

2 cups chopped broccoli or sliced cauliflower florets

⅓ cup chopped onion

⅓ cup chopped green bell pepper

1 cup shredded Cheddar cheese (4 ounces)

½ cup Original Bisquick® mix

1 cup milk

½ teaspoon salt

¼ teaspoon pepper

2 eggs

1 Heat oven to 400°F. Spray 9-inch glass pie plate with cooking spray. In medium saucepan, heat 1 inch water to boiling. Add broccoli. Cover; return to a boil. Cook about 5 minutes or until almost tender; drain thoroughly.

2 In pie plate, mix cooked broccoli, onion, bell pepper and cheese. In medium bowl, stir remaining ingredients until blended. Pour over mixture in pie plate.

3 Bake 35 to 45 minutes or until golden brown and knife inserted in center comes out clean. Cool 5 minutes.

1 Serving: Calories 180; Total Fat 10g (Saturated Fat 5g, Trans Fat 0g); Cholesterol 85mg; Sodium 460mg; Total Carbohydrate 13g (Dietary Fiber 1g); Protein 9g **Exchanges:** ½ Starch, ½ Vegetable, 1 High-Fat Meat, ½ Fat **Carbohydrate Choices:** 1

Customize It
For either the chopped broccoli or the cauliflower, you can substitute a frozen package of your choice instead of the fresh. One 10-ounce package is the correct amount for the substitution.

Impossibly Easy Ravioli Pie

FILLING

1   package (9 oz) refrigerated cheese-filled ravioli

1   cup chopped fresh spinach

⅓   cup chopped fresh basil leaves (about 1 oz)

1¼   cups tomato pasta sauce

1   cup shredded mozzarella cheese (4 oz)

CRUST

1   teaspoon vegetable oil

3   cloves garlic, finely chopped

½   cup Original Bisquick® mix

1   cup milk

2   eggs

¼   cup shredded Parmesan cheese (1 oz)

TOPPING

2   cups tomato pasta sauce, heated

1   Heat oven to 400°F. Grease bottom only of 9-inch glass pie plate with shortening or cooking spray.

2   Place half of ravioli in bottom of pie plate. Sprinkle with spinach and basil. Spoon 1 cup of the pasta sauce over top; sprinkle with ½ cup of the mozzarella cheese. Layer with remaining ravioli. Top with remaining ½ cup mozzarella cheese and remaining ¼ cup pasta sauce.

3   In 8-inch skillet, heat oil over medium heat. Cook and stir garlic in oil until fragrant, about 1 minute. In medium bowl, stir garlic, Bisquick mix, milk, eggs and Parmesan cheese with fork. Pour evenly over filling in pie plate.

4   Bake uncovered 30 to 35 minutes or until crust is browned and filling is bubbly. Let stand 5 minutes before cutting. Serve with heated pasta sauce.

1 Serving: Calories 400; Total Fat 18g (Saturated Fat 7g, Trans Fat 0.5g); Cholesterol 135mg; Sodium 1310mg; Total Carbohydrate 42g (Dietary Fiber 2g); Protein 16g **Exchanges:** 1½ Starch, 1 Other Carbohydrate, 1 Vegetable, 1 Medium-Fat Meat, 2½ Fat **Carbohydrate Choices:** 3

Make It a Meal This dish is ravioli and garlic bread in one! To continue the Italian flavors, serve with steamed green beans tossed in Italian dressing.

Customize It No need to stick with plain cheese ravioli— experiment with different flavors. Try various pasta sauces, too, to find your favorite combination.

Metric Conversion Guide

VOLUME

U.S. UNITS	CANADIAN METRIC	AUSTRALIAN METRIC
¼ teaspoon	1 mL	1 ml
½ teaspoon	2 mL	2 ml
1 teaspoon	5 mL	5 ml
1 tablespoon	15 mL	20 ml
¼ cup	50 mL	60 ml
⅓ cup	75 mL	80 ml
½ cup	125 mL	125 ml
⅔ cup	150 mL	170 ml
¾ cup	175 mL	190 ml
1 cup	250 mL	250 ml
1 quart	1 liter	1 liter
1½ quarts	1.5 liters	1.5 liters
2 quarts	2 liters	2 liters
2½ quarts	2.5 liters	2.5 liters
3 quarts	3 liters	3 liters
4 quarts	4 liters	4 liters

WEIGHT

U.S. UNITS	CANADIAN METRIC	AUSTRALIAN METRIC
1 ounce	30 grams	30 grams
2 ounces	55 grams	60 grams
3 ounces	85 grams	90 grams
4 ounces (¼ pound)	115 grams	125 grams
8 ounces (½ pound)	225 grams	225 grams
16 ounces (1 pound)	455 grams	500 grams
1 pound	455 grams	0.5 kilogram

Note: The recipes in this cookbook have not been developed or tested using metric measures. When converting recipes to metric, some variations in quality may be noted.

MEASUREMENTS

INCHES	CENTIMETERS
1	2.5
2	5.0
3	7.5
4	10.0
5	12.5
6	15.0
7	17.5
8	20.5
9	23.0
10	25.5
11	28.0
12	30.5
13	33.0

TEMPERATURES

FAHRENHEIT	CELSIUS
32°	0°
212°	100°
250°	120°
275°	140°
300°	150°
325°	160°
350°	180°
375°	190°
400°	200°
425°	220°
450°	230°
475°	240°
500°	260°

Index

NOTE: Page reference in *italics* refer to photos.

Recipe Testing and Calculating Nutrition Information

RECIPE TESTING:

- Large eggs and 2% milk were used unless otherwise indicated.

- Fat-free, low-fat, low-sodium or lite products were not used unless indicated.

- No nonstick cookware and bakeware were used unless otherwise indicated. No dark-colored, black or insulated bakeware was used.

- When a pan is specified, a metal pan was used; a baking dish or pie plate means ovenproof glass was used.

- An electric hand mixer was used for mixing only when mixer speeds are specified.

CALCULATING NUTRITION:

- The first ingredient was used wherever a choice is given, such as 1/3 cup sour cream or plain yogurt.

- The first amount was used wherever a range is given, such as 3- to 3½-pound whole chicken.

- The first serving number was used wherever a range is given, such as 4 to 6 servings.

- "If desired" ingredients were not included.

- Only the amount of a marinade or frying oil that is absorbed was included.